ED EMBERLEY'S
BIG RED
DRAWING BOOK

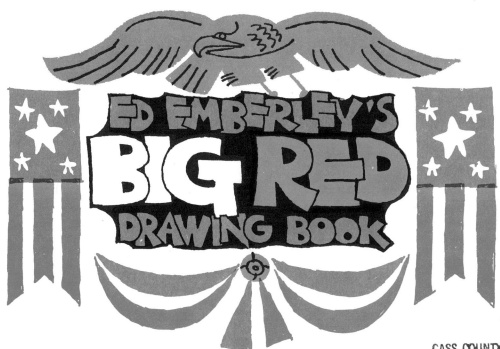

ED EMBERLEY'S BIG RED DRAWING BOOK

LITTLE, BROWN AND COMPANY / BOSTON

★FIRST EDITION

LIBRARY OF CONGRESS
CATALOGING-IN-PUBLICATION DATA

EMBERLEY, ED.
    ED EMBERLEY'S BIG RED DRAWING BOOK

    SUMMARY: PRESENTS STEP-BY-STEP INSTRUCTIONS
FOR DRAWING PEOPLE, ANIMALS AND OBJECTS
USING A MINIMUM OF LINE AND CIRCLE COMBINATIONS.
    1. DRAWING--TECHNIQUE--JUVENILE LITERATURE.
[1. DRAWING--TECHNIQUE] I. TITLE. II. TITLE: BIG
RED DRAWING BOOK.

NC730.E64 1987   741.2'6   87-3091
ISBN 0-316-23434-6
ISBN 0-316-23435-4 (PBK.)
HC: 10 9 8 7 6 5 4 3
PB: 20 19 18 17 16 15 14 13 12

WOR

PRINTED IN THE UNITED STATES OF AMERICA

THIS IS A WRITING ALPHABET.

ABCDEFGHIJKLMNOPQRSTUVWXYZ

YOU CAN USE IT TO MAKE WORDS.

CAT

THIS IS A DRAWING ALPHABET.

YOU CAN USE IT TO MAKE PICTURES

HERE'S HOW....THIS ROW SHOWS <u>WHAT</u> TO DRAW, THIS ROW SHOWS WHERE TO PUT IT.

THIS SYMBOL MEANS "FILL IN."

CAT

RED IS A JUST-RIGHT COLOR FOR DRAWING LOTS OF THINGS, SUCH AS :

RED ANTS, · MEASLES, CRANBERRIES, HOLLY BERRIES, CHECKERS,

CHERRY OR STRAWBERRY LOLLIPOPS, JAPANESE FLAGS, RED-CROSS FLAGS, DANGER FLAGS

CHERRIES,

STRAW-BERRIES,

TOMATOES,

RADISHES,

APPLES,

TULIPS,

ROSES.

PINK

(LIGHT RED) IS A JUST-RIGHT COLOR FOR DRAWING A FEW THINGS

SUCH AS: BUBBLE GUM, CHEEKS, NOSES, STRAWBERRY ICE CREAM,

SUNDAE,

WATERMELON,

ALSO

BUBBLE,

PINK ELEPHANT.

RED WHITE AND BLUE

ARE JUST-RIGHT COLORS FOR DRAWING AMERICAN AND OTHER FLAGS
AND THINGS SUCH AS:

FIRECRACKERS

ROCKETS,

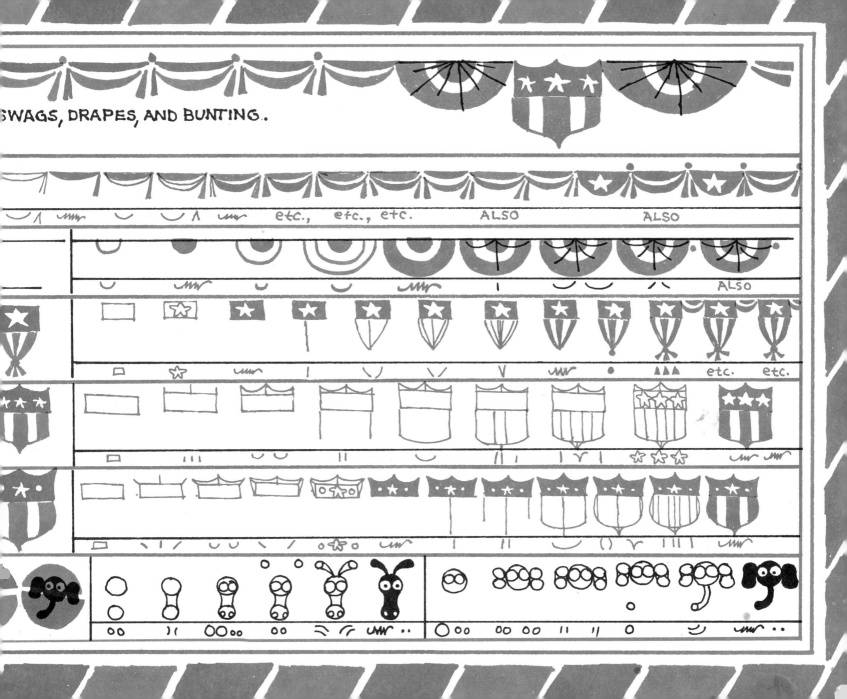

SWAGS, DRAPES, AND BUNTING..

etc., etc., etc.   ALSO   ALSO

ALSO

etc.   etc.

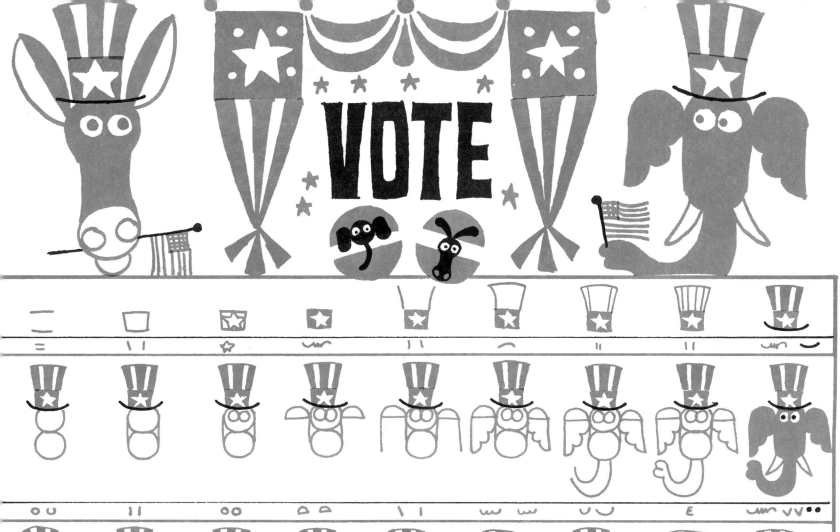

LIBERTY BELL

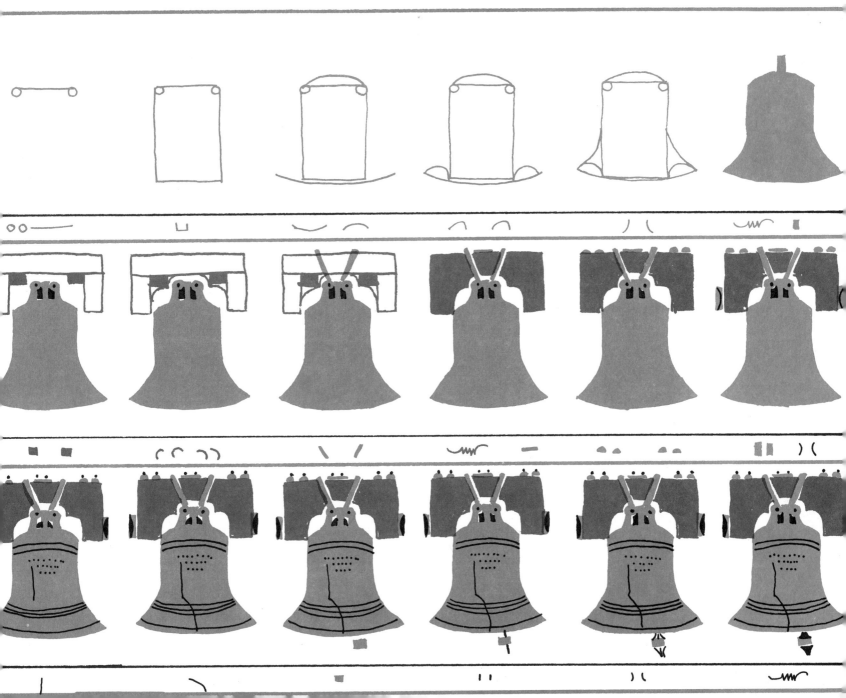

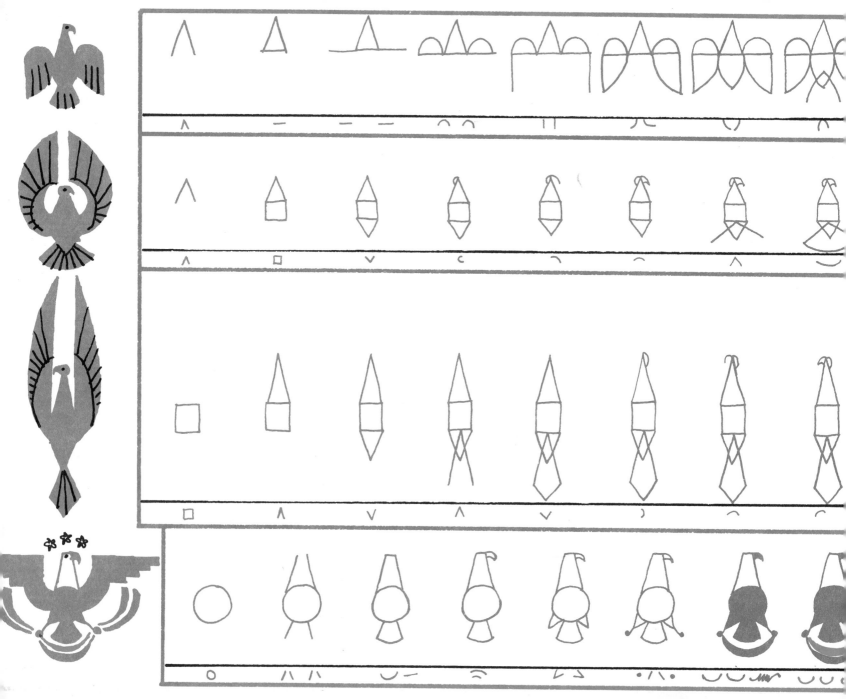

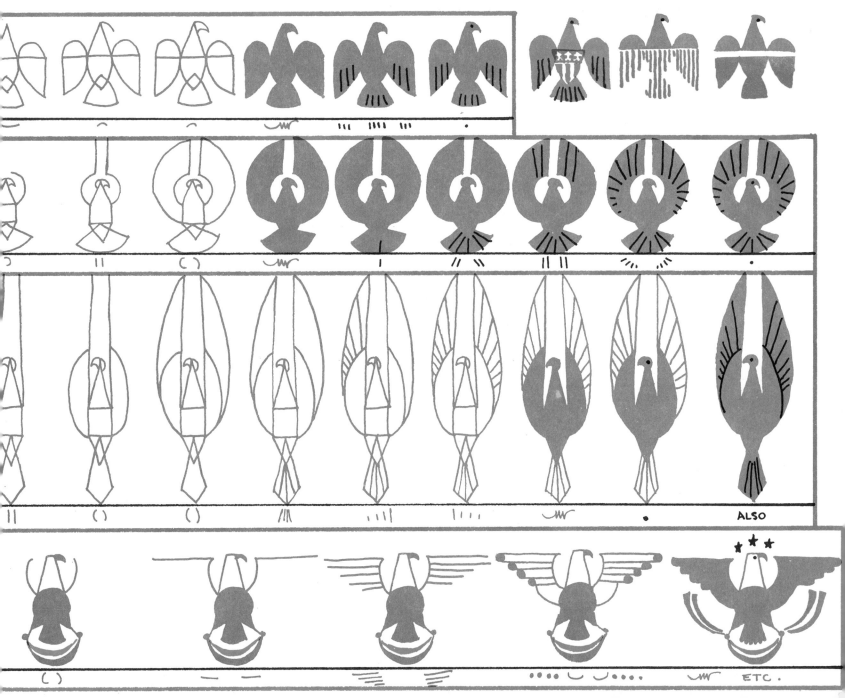

ALSO

ETC.

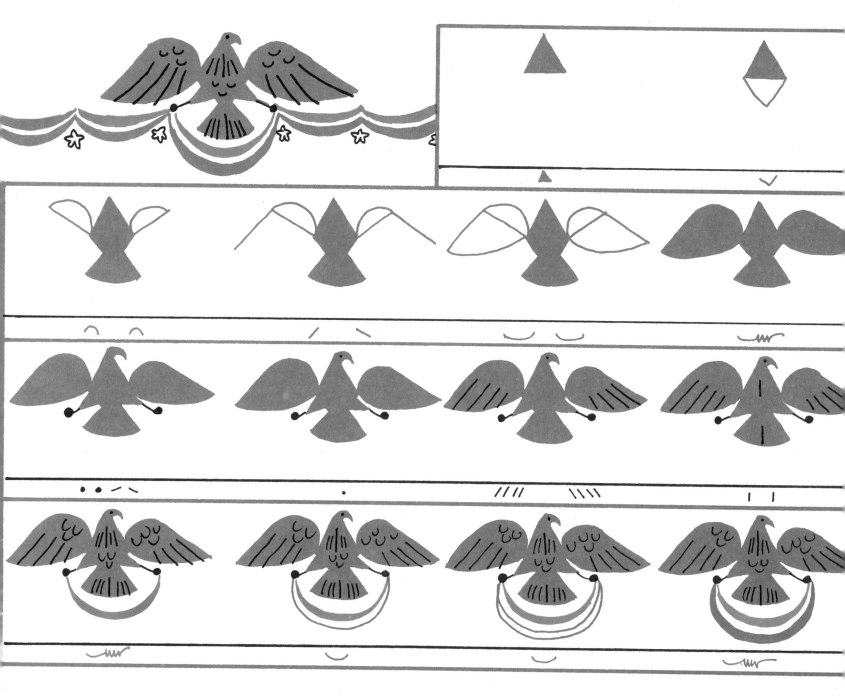

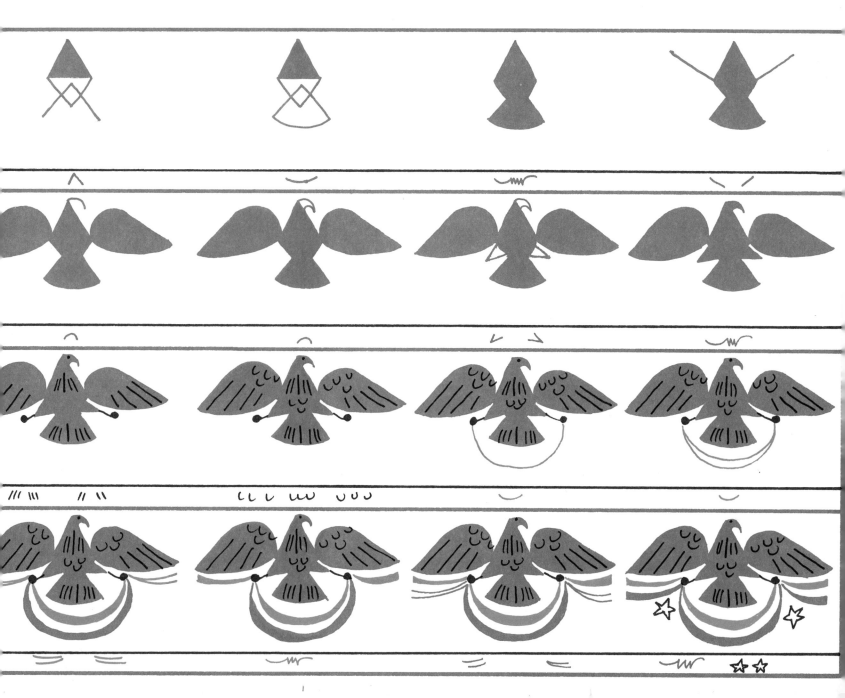

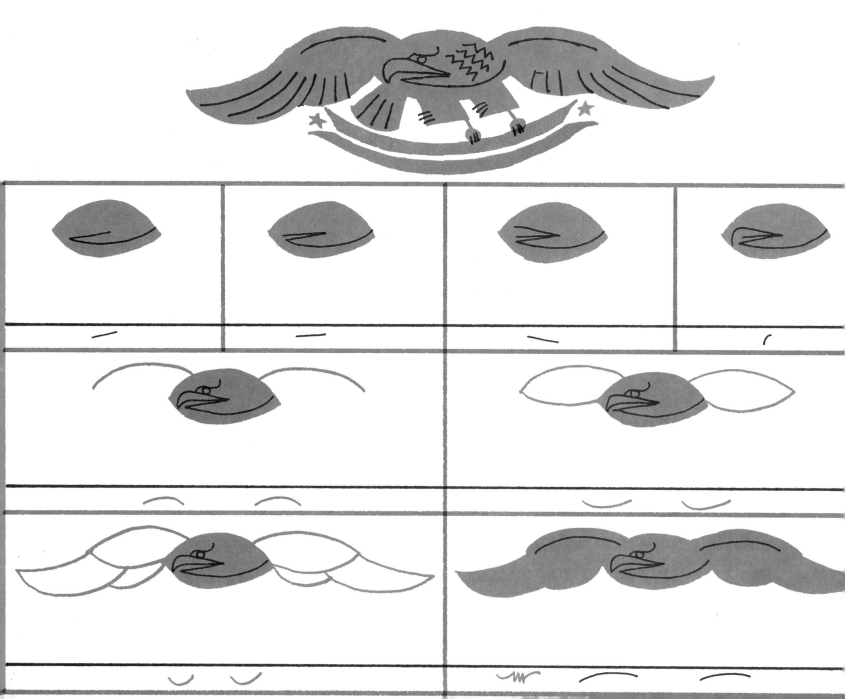

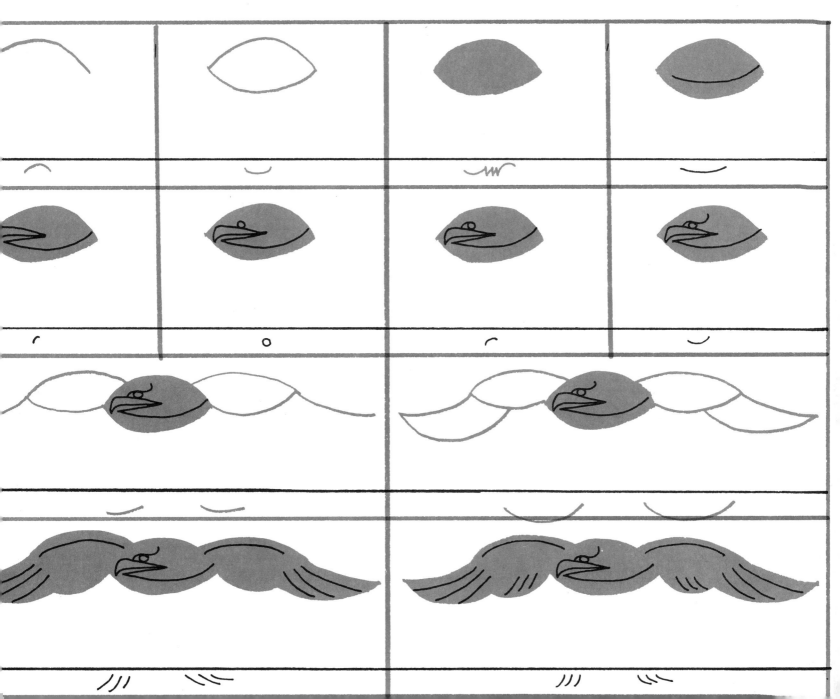

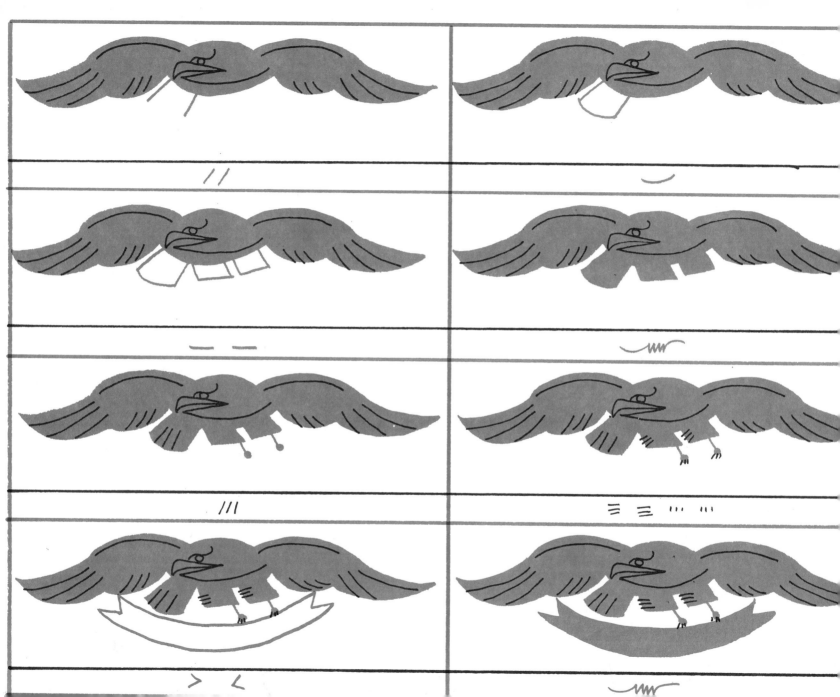

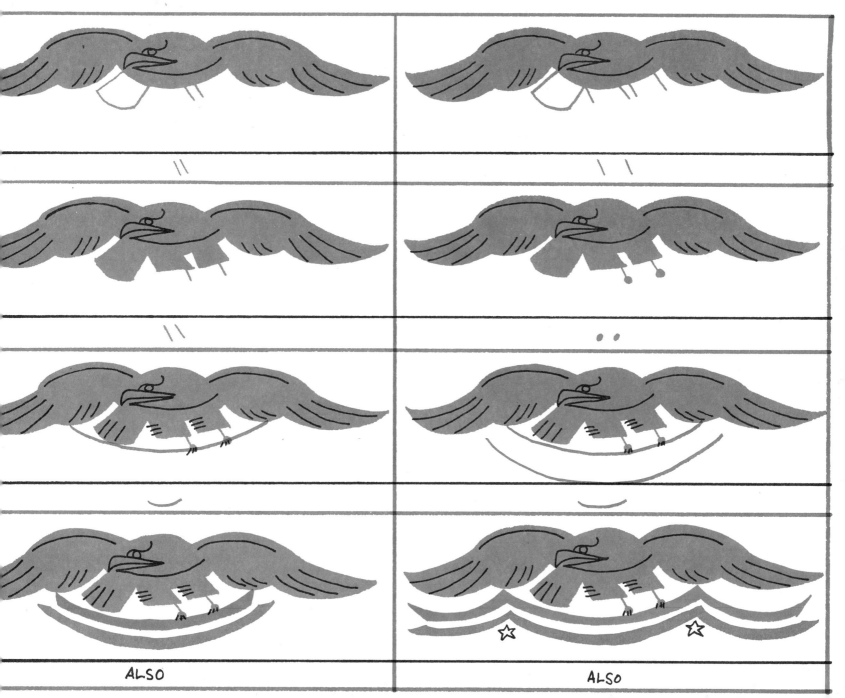

ALSO   ALSO

STARS AND STRIPES

FIRST, THE STRIPES, NOT **TOO** COMPLICATED. (13 STRIPES ⁓ 7 RED, 6 WHITE)

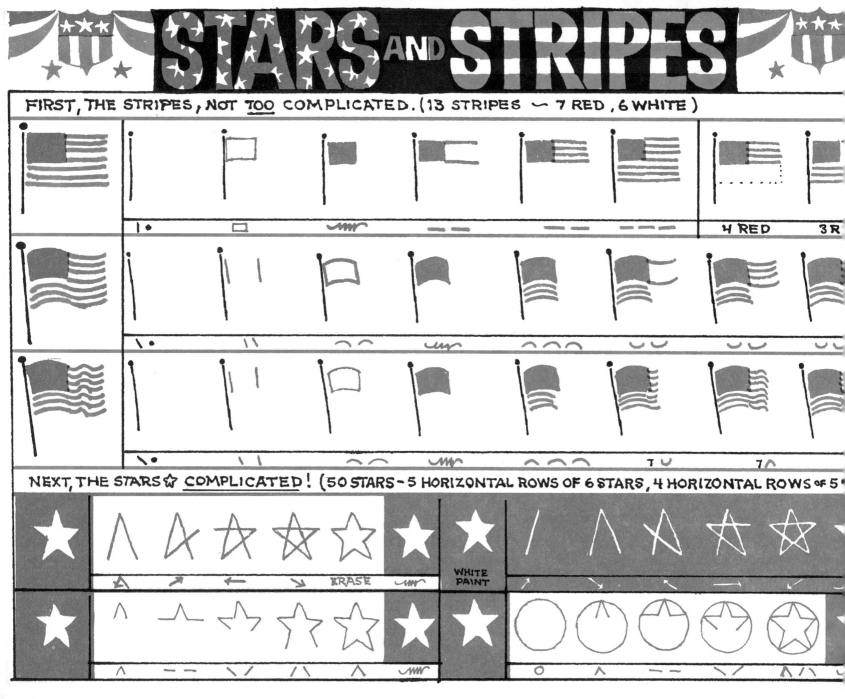

4 RED   3 R

NEXT, THE STARS ✩ **COMPLICATED**! (50 STARS – 5 HORIZONTAL ROWS OF 6 STARS, 4 HORIZONTAL ROWS OF 5

ERASE

WHITE PAINT

THE CANTON (THE BLUE RECTANGLE WITH ITS FULL SET OF 50 STARS)

FIRST, A SIMPLE METHOD, GOOD FOR DRAWING SMALL AND/OR FARAWAY FLAGS.

CANTON II (FOR STAR COUNTERS)

FOR DRAWING BIGGER AND/OR CLOSER FLAGS.

GUIDELINES

4 3 2 1

1 2 3 4

1

ONE ROW OF 5 — ONE ROW OF 4 — REPEAT 4 MORE TIMES — PLUS ONE ROW OF 5 —

DRAW STARS —   FILL IN.

CANTON III

STARS IN CANTON ARE ACTUALLY SET IN A GRID LIKE THIS (SEE NEXT PAGE). TO CREATE THIS ILLUSION, MAKE STARS LIKE THIS.

FLAG WILL SEEM TO WAVE IF CURVED GUIDELINES ARE USED.

CANTON IV — THE STARS IN THE CANTON ARE PLACED WITHIN A GRID THAT IS WIDER THAN IT IS HIGH. TO MAKE THIS SPECIAL GRID YOU MUST FIRST LEARN HOW TO "TIC AND TRY."

THE TOOLS — A "TIC STRIP" (ANY STRIP OF PAPER WITH ONE STRAIGHT EDGE.) A COMPASS, A TRIANGLE (OR AN OLD PAD BACK).

TIC STRIP

THE METHOD — "TIC AND TRY" IS A PRACTICAL, PROFESSIONAL METHOD THAT CAN BE USED TO DIVIDE A LINE INTO ANY NUMBER OF EQUAL PARTS, WITHOUT MAT

FOR INSTANCE, HERE'S HOW TO DIVIDE THIS LINE INTO 3 EQUAL PARTS.

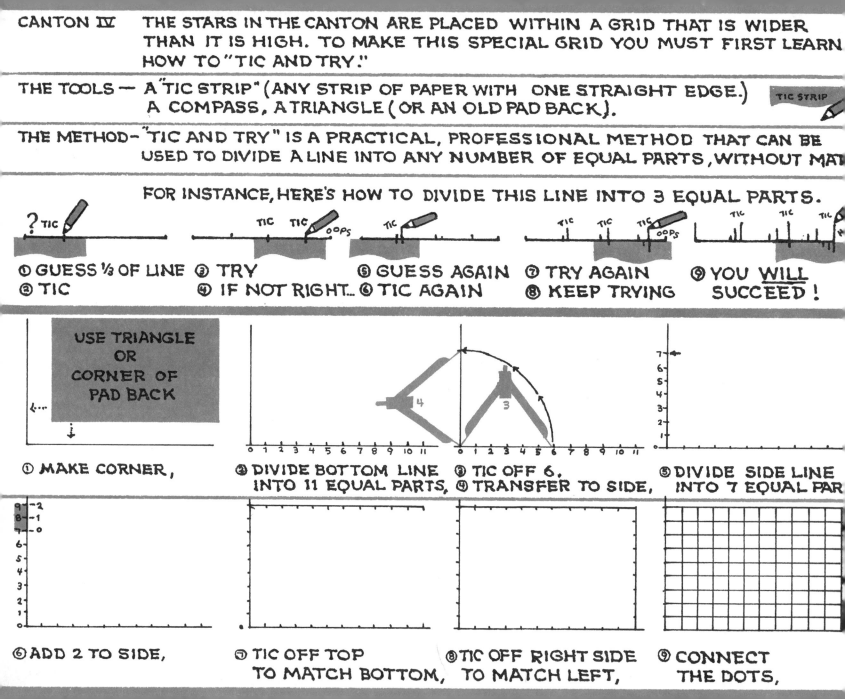

① GUESS ⅓ OF LINE ③ TRY ⑤ GUESS AGAIN ⑦ TRY AGAIN ⑨ YOU WILL
② TIC ④ IF NOT RIGHT... ⑥ TIC AGAIN ⑧ KEEP TRYING SUCCEED !

USE TRIANGLE OR CORNER OF PAD BACK

① MAKE CORNER,

② DIVIDE BOTTOM LINE INTO 11 EQUAL PARTS,

③ TIC OFF 6, ④ TRANSFER TO SIDE,

⑤ DIVIDE SIDE LINE INTO 7 EQUAL PAR

⑥ ADD 2 TO SIDE,

⑦ TIC OFF TOP TO MATCH BOTTOM,

⑧ TIC OFF RIGHT SIDE TO MATCH LEFT,

⑨ CONNECT THE DOTS,

⑩ **CRISS CROSS,**
(START IN CORNER)

⑪ **EVERY OTHER SPACE,**

⑫ **LINES,**
(X TO X)

BORDER IS ON ALL 4 SIDES

½

SAME

CIRCLE, ⑭ **DIVIDE, 5 PARTS** ⑮ **DOT-TO-DOT,** ⑯ **OUTLINE** ⑰ **FILL, ERASE,**

NOTE-FILL IN OUTSIDE OUTLINE.

5 2
4 3

⑱ **CANTON HAS BLUE BORDER. IT IS ½ THE WIDTH OF A STAR SPACE**

FOR MORE STAR TALK AND LARGE CANTON SEE NEXT PAGE →

CANTON IV

1 2 3 4 5 6 7

1 2 3 4 5 6

EXTEND LINES, ⑳ **DIVIDE, 7 EQUAL PARTS,** ㉑ **TIC OFF 6,** ㉒ **TIC OFF WIDTH,** (SAME AS CANTON)

SAME

MAKE CORNER, ㉔ **TIC OFF 13,**

1 2 3 4 5 6 7 8 9 10 11 12 13

㉕ **DRAW LINES,** ——— ㉖ **FILL IN**
(DOT-TO-DOT) ㉗ **CONGRATULATE YOURSELF!**

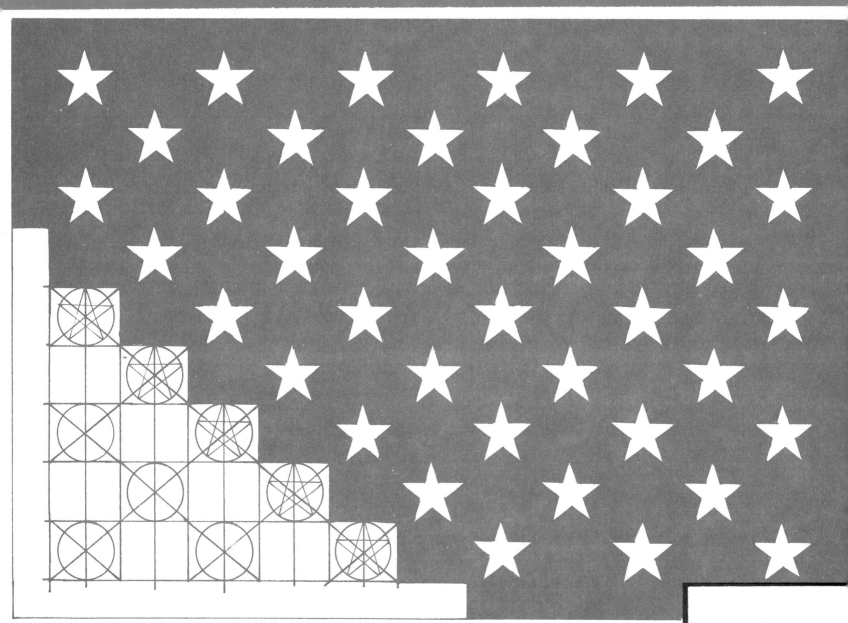

ACCURACY–DIFFICULT IN SMALL SIZES THE LARGER THE EASIER
CANTON V–A FURTHER REFINEMENT, STAR POINTS SHOULD TOUCH
TOP AND BOTTOM OF STAR BOX (BUT NOT THE SIDES).

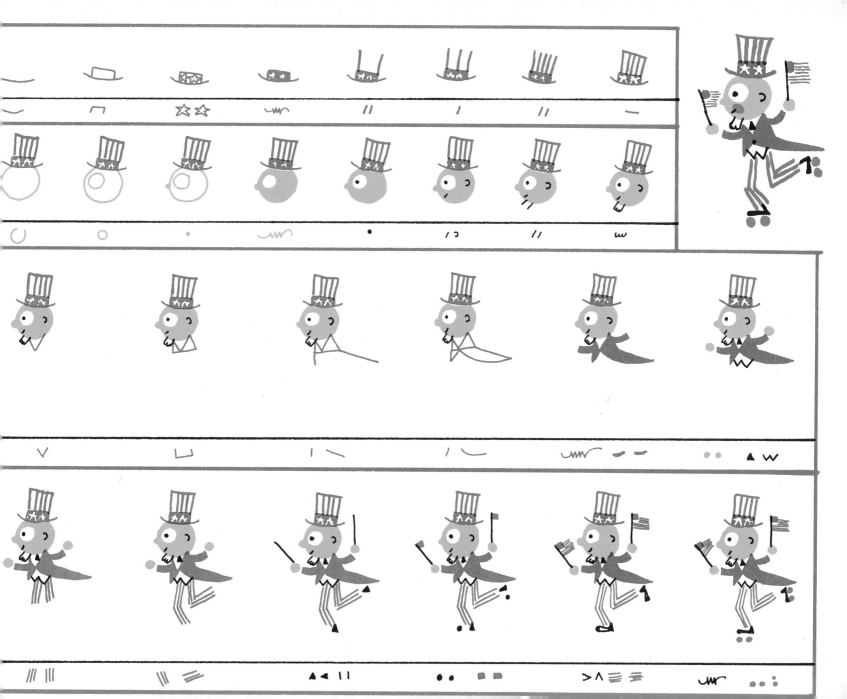

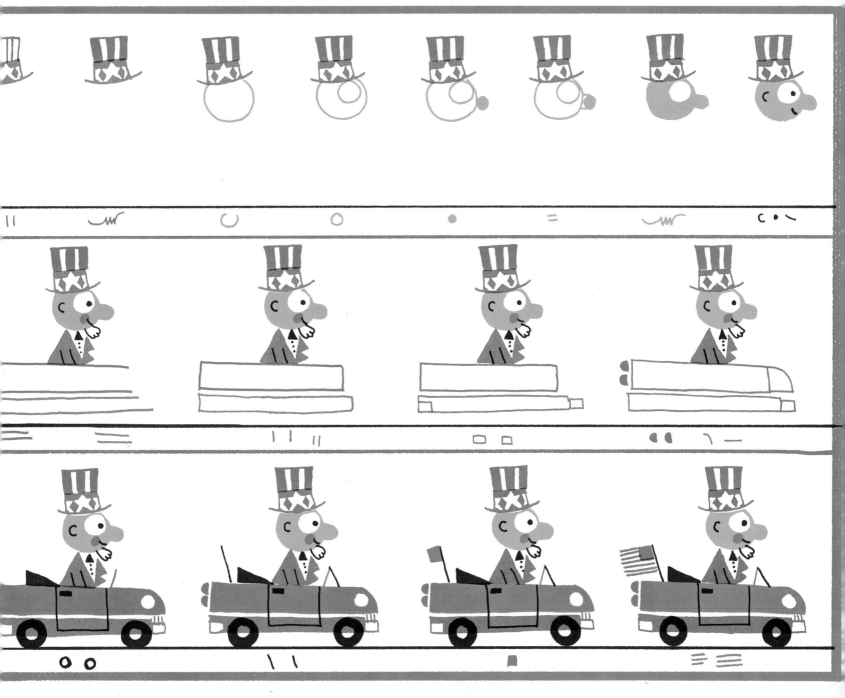

VALENTINE'S DAY

								HAPPY HEART		RUNNING						

LOVEBUG

LOVEBIRD

VALENTINE

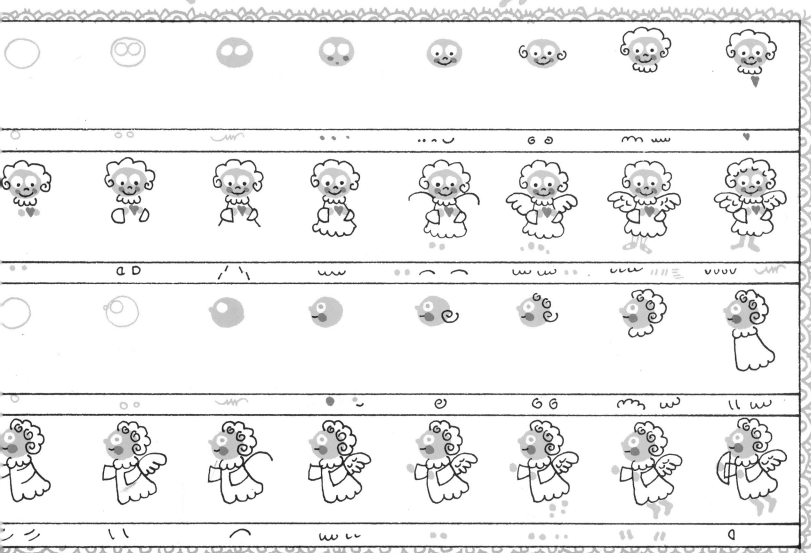

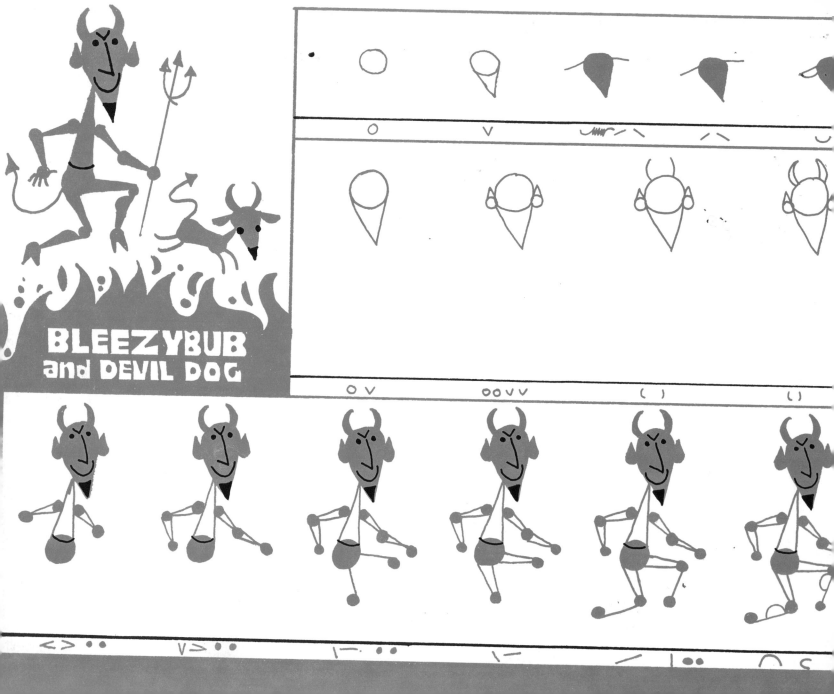

BLEEZYBUB and DEVIL DOG

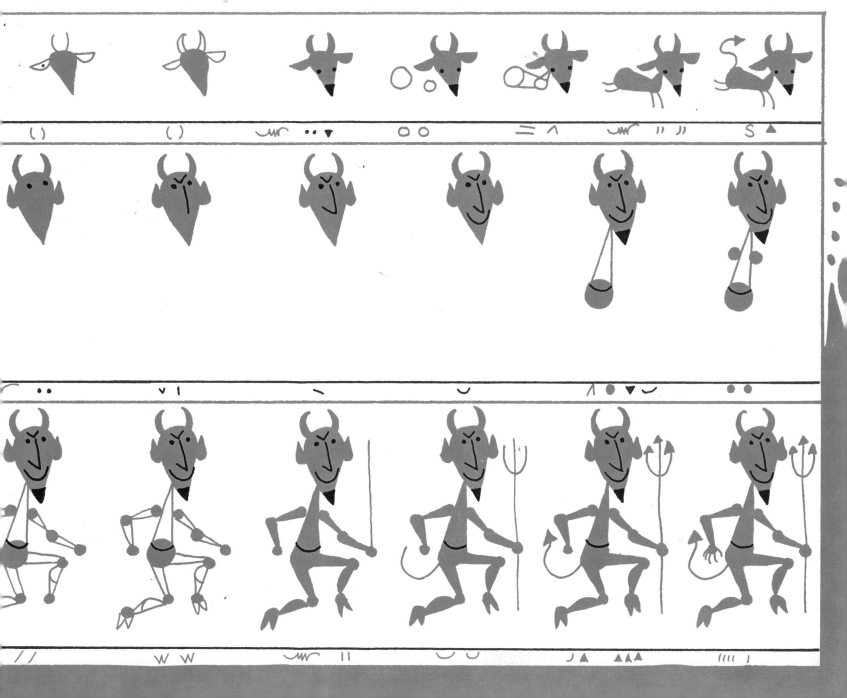

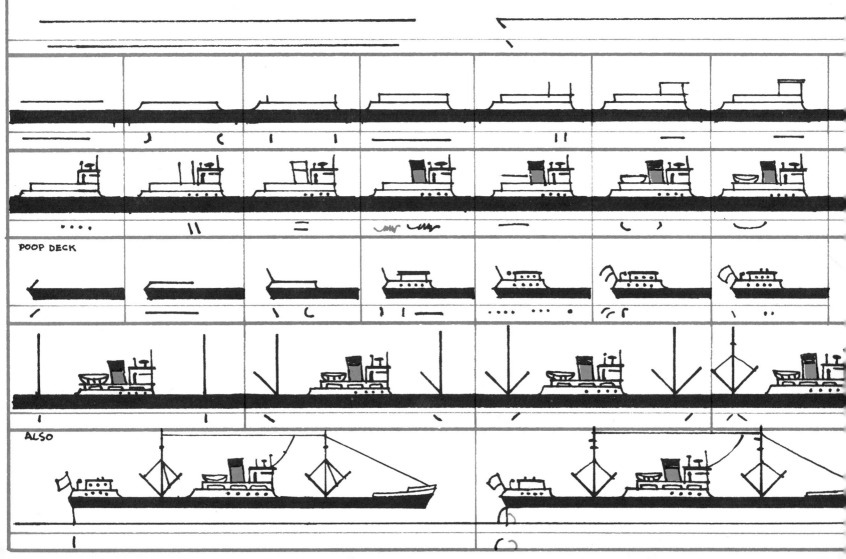

CARGO SHIPS

FREIGHTER / OCEAN-GOING SHIP, VARIOUS CARGOES.

COASTER / SHORT TRIPS ALONG THE COA

POOP DECK

ALSO

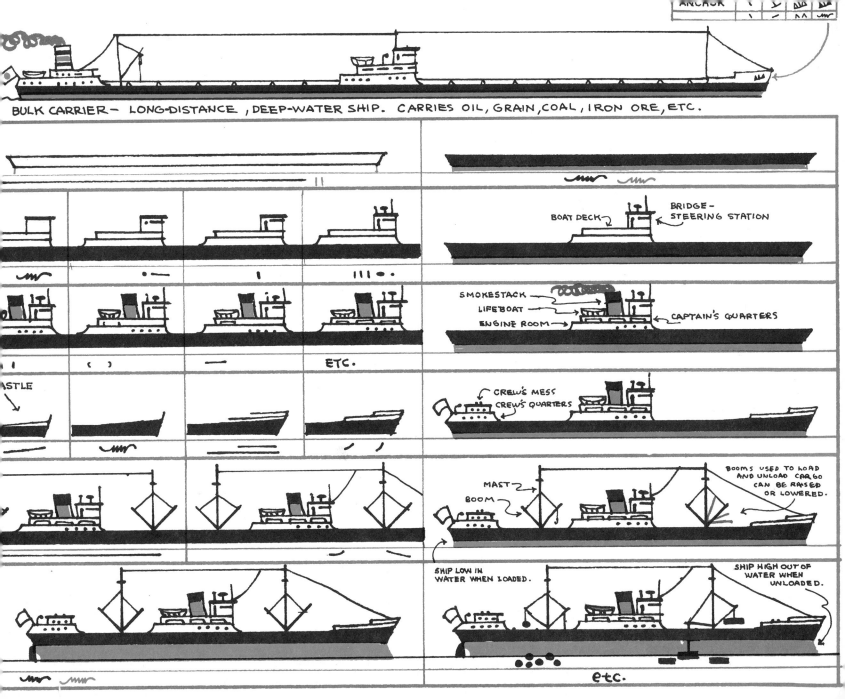

BULK CARRIER— LONG-DISTANCE, DEEP-WATER SHIP. CARRIES OIL, GRAIN, COAL, IRON ORE, ETC.

BOAT DECK
BRIDGE—
STEERING STATION

SMOKESTACK
LIFEBOAT
ENGINE ROOM
CAPTAIN'S QUARTERS

ETC.

...STLE

CREW'S MESS
CREW'S QUARTERS

BOOMS USED TO LOAD
AND UNLOAD CARGO
CAN BE RAISED
OR LOWERED.

MAST
BOOM

SHIP LOW IN
WATER WHEN LOADED.

SHIP HIGH OUT OF
WATER WHEN
UNLOADED.

etc.

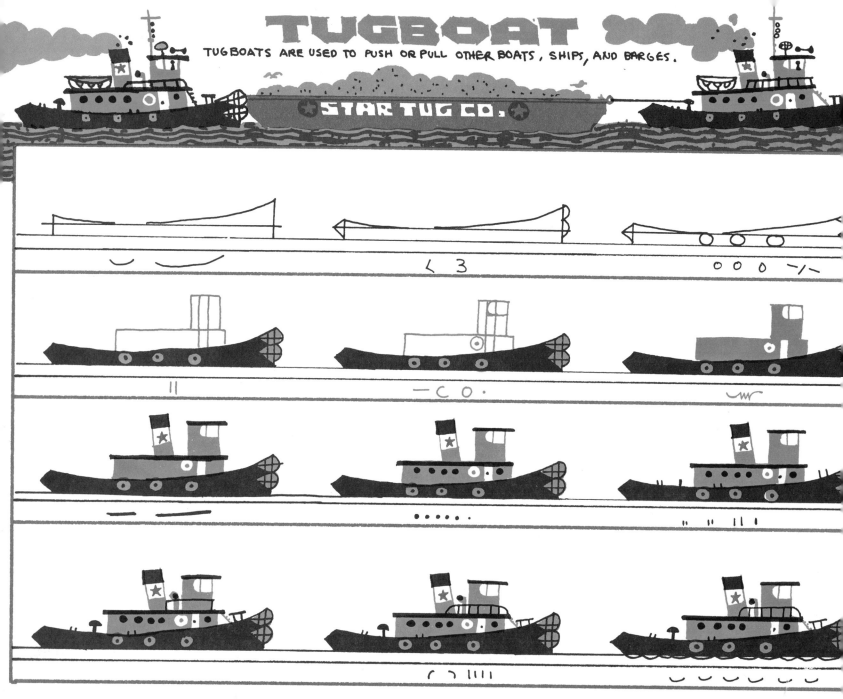

TUGBOAT

TUGBOATS ARE USED TO PUSH OR PULL OTHER BOATS, SHIPS, AND BARGES.

STAR TUG CO.

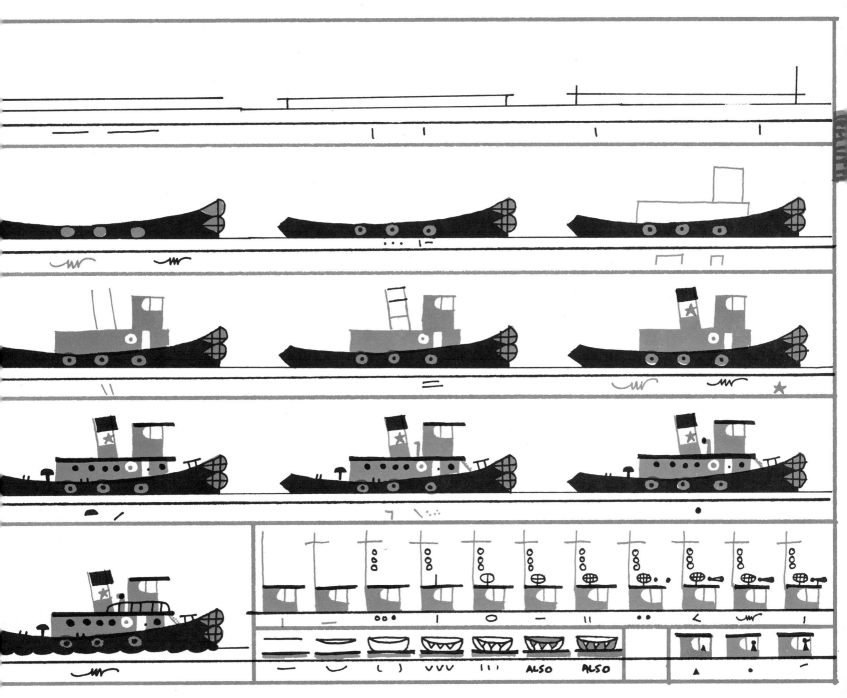

LIGHTSHIP

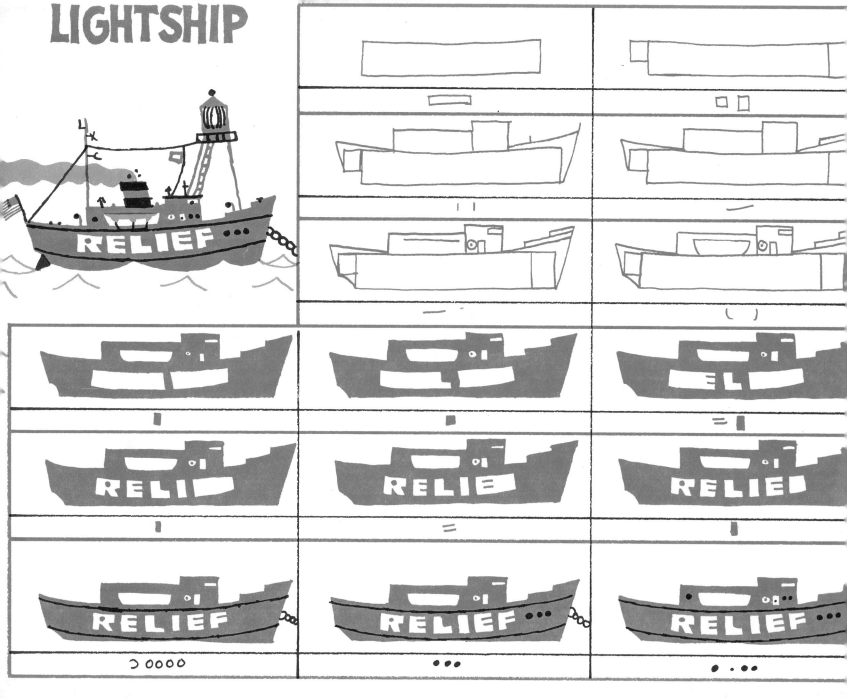

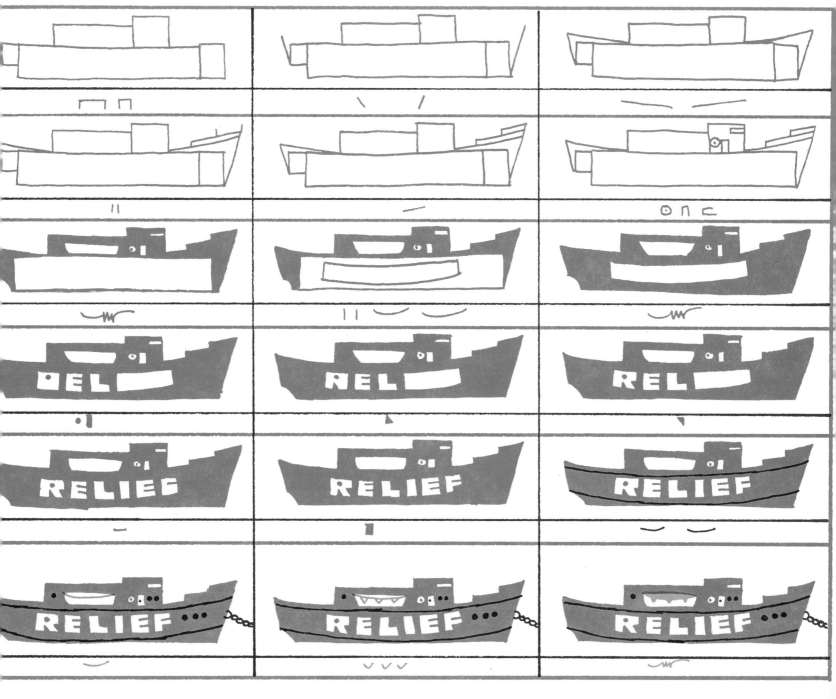

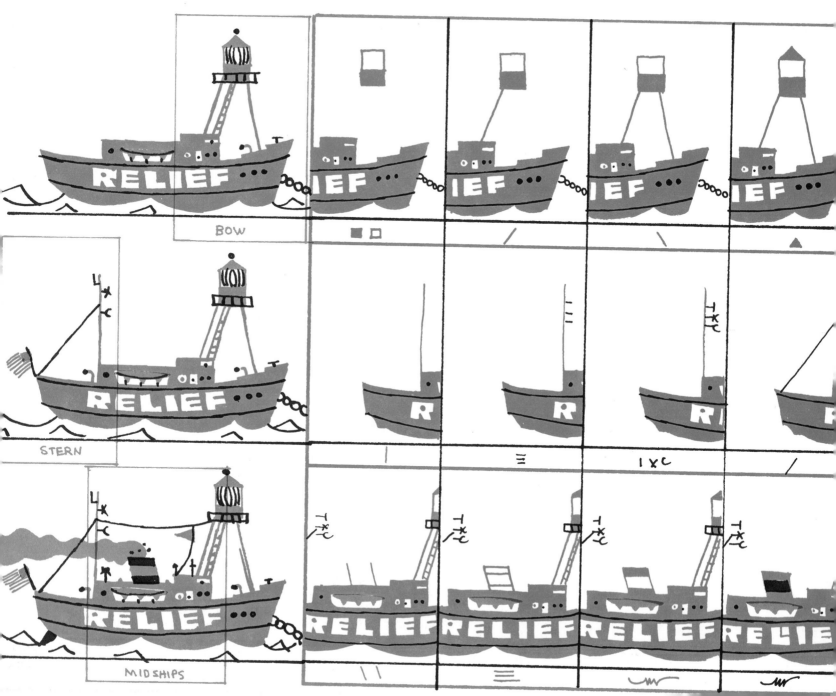

BOW

STERN

MIDSHIPS

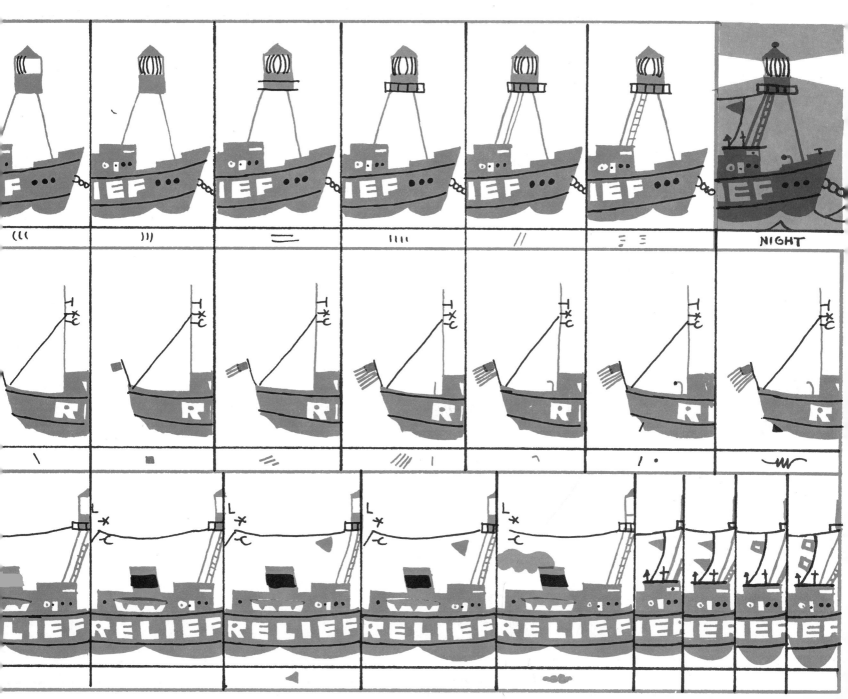

POLICE CRUISER

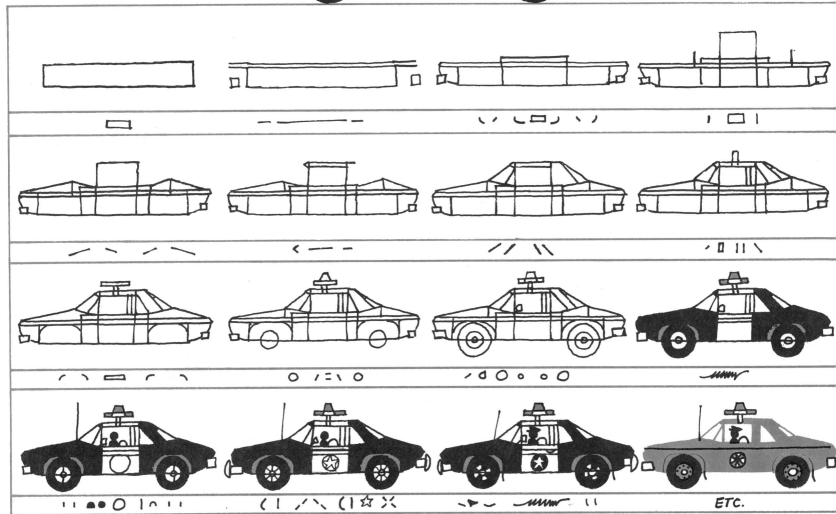

ETC.

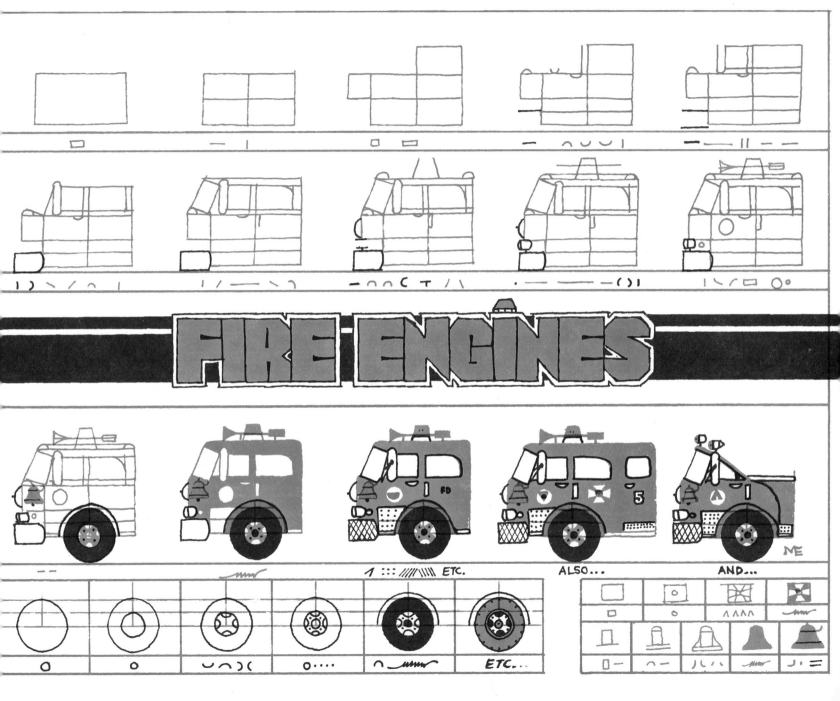

FIRE ENGINES

1 ::: //////\\\\ ETC.

ALSO...

AND...

--

o ∪∩)(o.... ETC...

ME

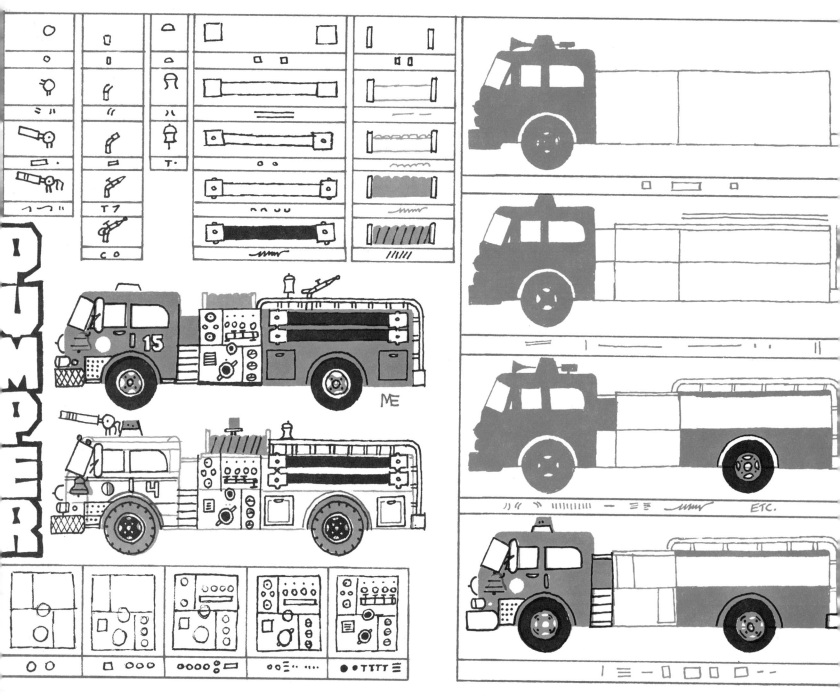

SNORKEL

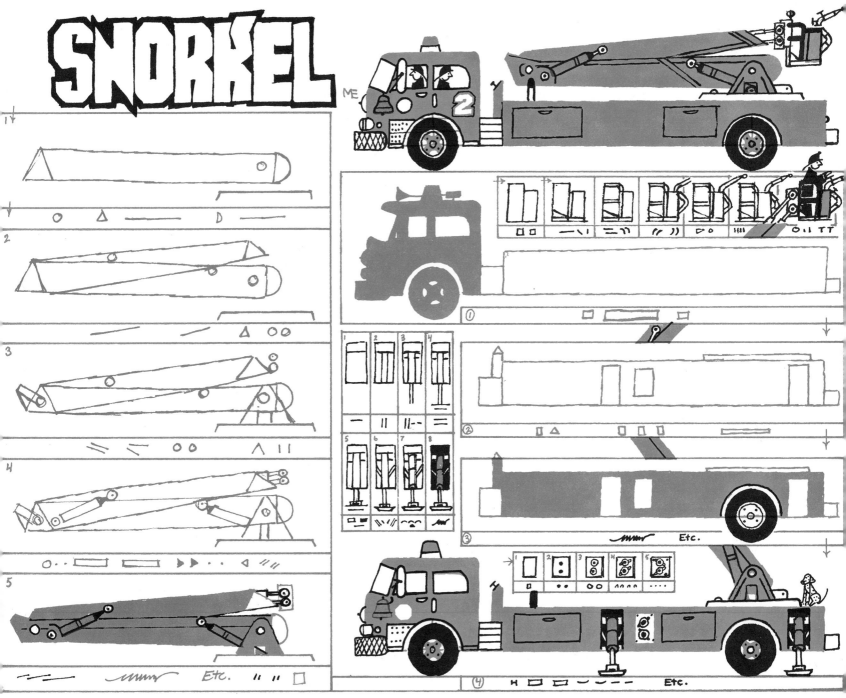

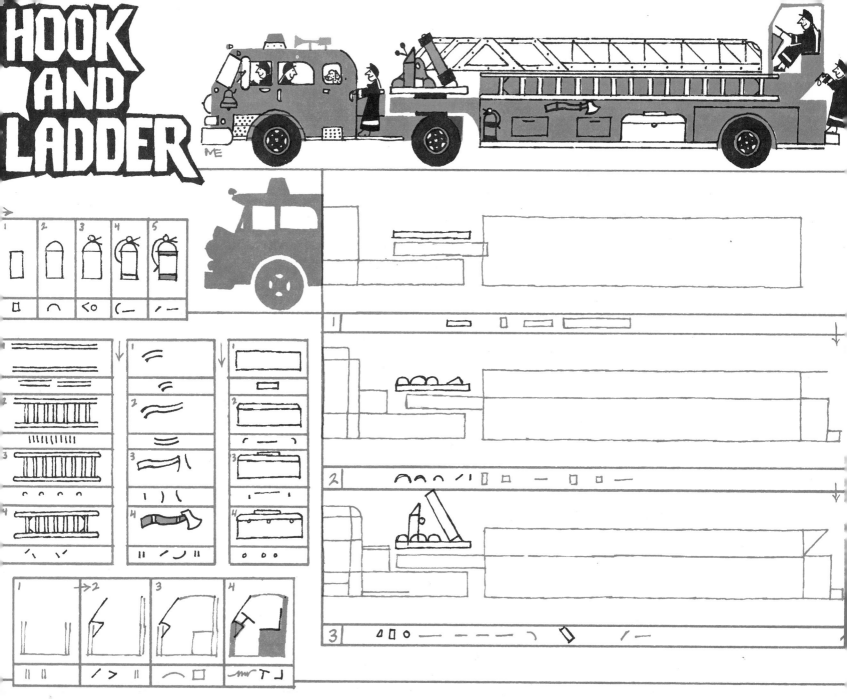

HOOK AND LADDER

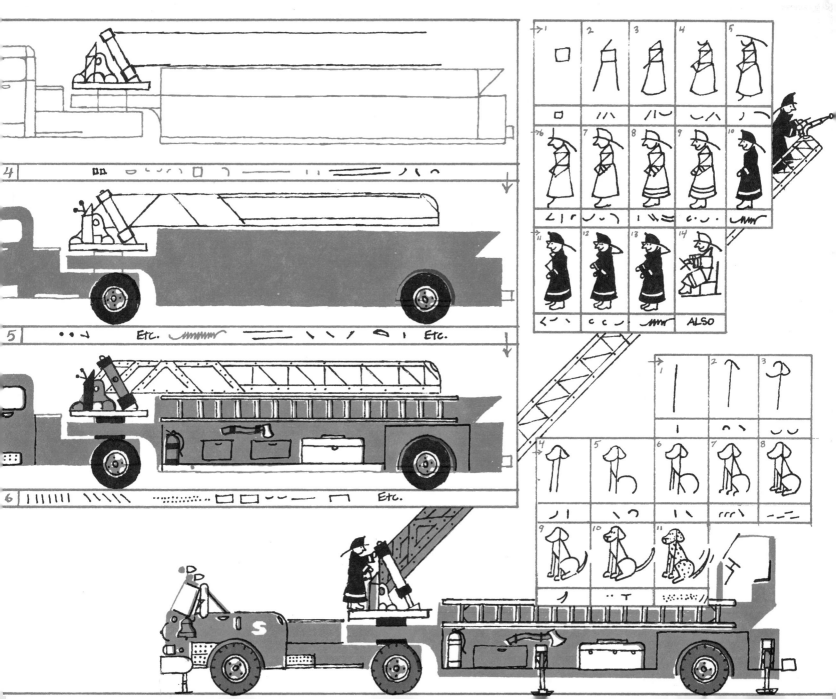

FEEDLE

FOODLE AS SEEN FRO

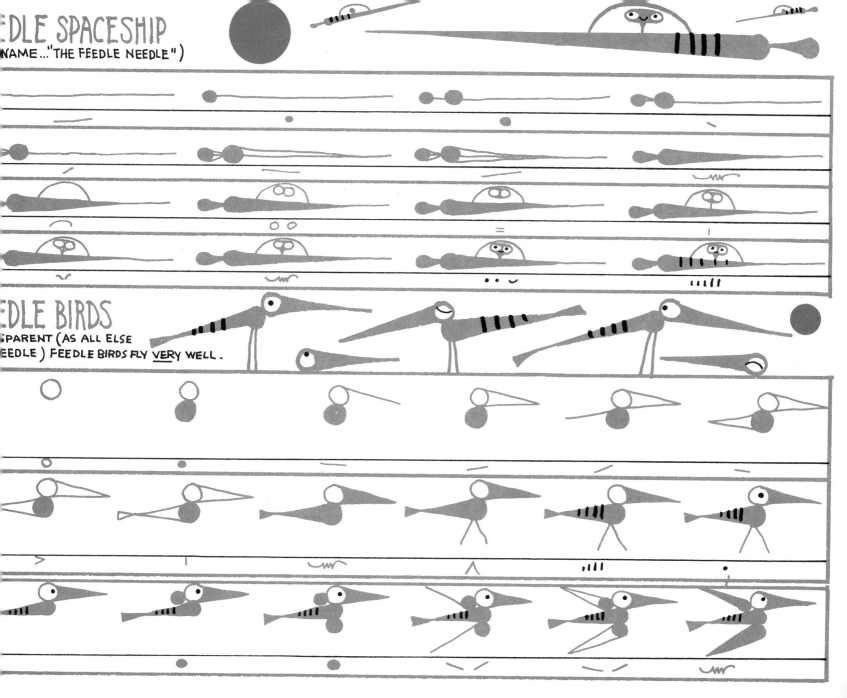

EDLE SPACESHIP
(NAME..."THE FEEDLE NEEDLE")

EDLE BIRDS
SPARENT (AS ALL ELSE
EEDLE) FEEDLE BIRDS FLY <u>VERY</u> WELL.

FOODLE

FOODLE AND FEEDLE ARE THE TWIN MOONS OF PLANET ZORT. (ZORT IN <u>BIG GREEN DRAWING BOOK.</u>)

FOODLER

FOODLE PET

FEEDLE AS SEEN FROM FOODLE

·DLE SPACESHIP

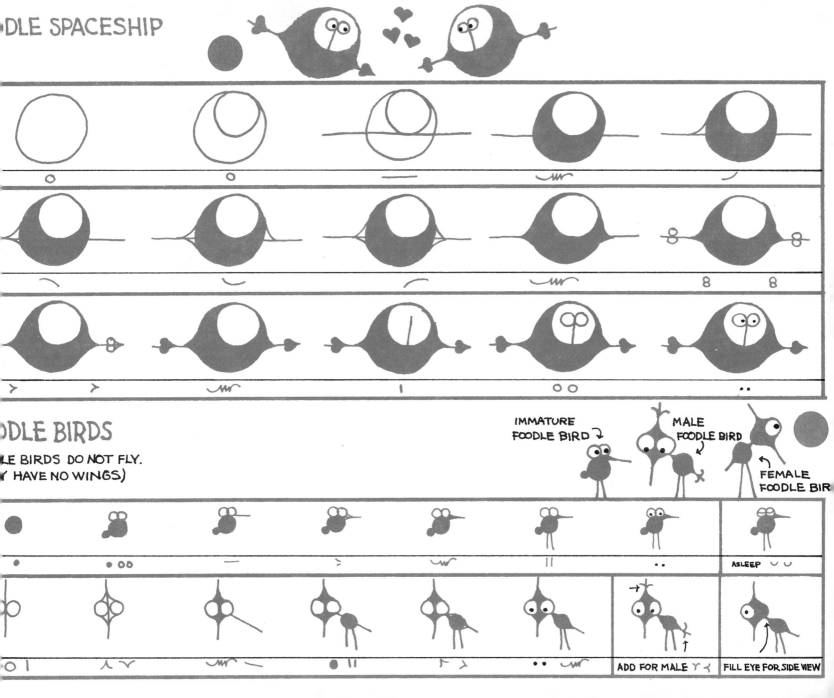

·DLE BIRDS

·LE BIRDS DO NOT FLY.
(·Y HAVE NO WINGS)

IMMATURE
FOODLE BIRD ↳

MALE
FOODLE BIRD ↙

FEMALE
FOODLE BIR·

ASLEEP ∪ ∪

ADD FOR MALE Υ ⋊

FILL EYE FOR SIDE VIEW

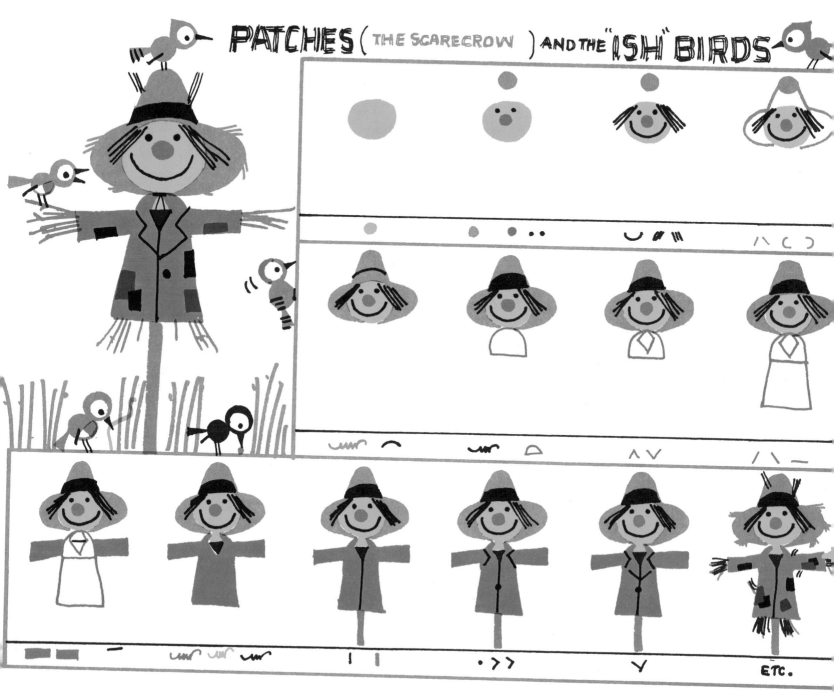

PATCHES (THE SCARECROW) AND THE "ISH" BIRDS

ETC.

("ISH" BIRDS ARE SMALL IMAGINARY BIRDS THAT REMIND YOU OF CERTAIN REAL BIRDS.)

JAY   JAYISH BIRD   ROBINISH BIRD   ROBIN

BLUE BIRDISH RT OF A BIRD

JAYISH RT OF A BIRD

CARDINALISH RT OF A BIRD

ROBINISH RT OF A BIRD

BROWN

CROWISH RT OF A BIRD

OODPECKERISH RT OF A BIRD

THE PEANUT GALLERY

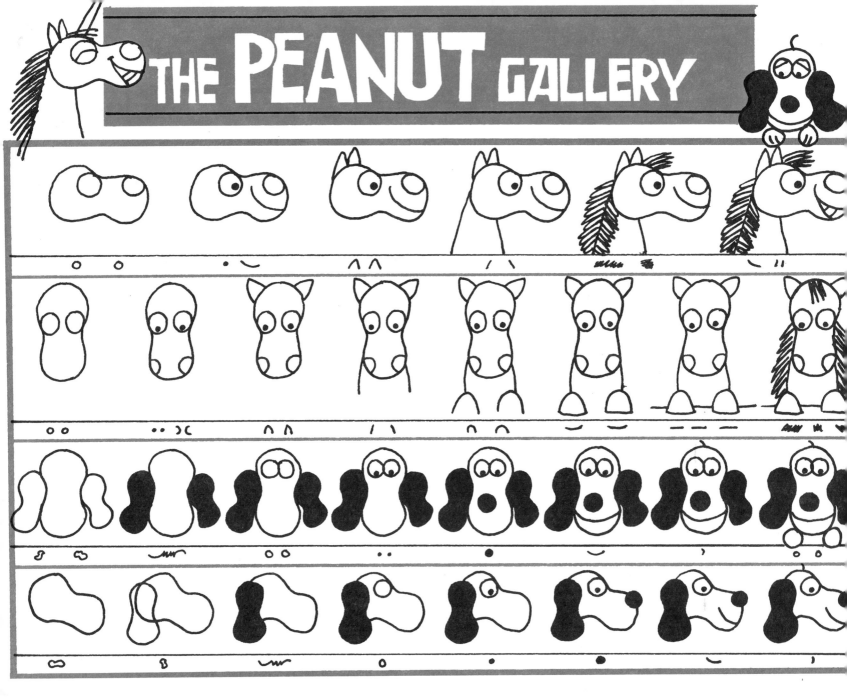

TWO WAYS TO DRAW A PEANUT.

RUNNING

RABBITS!

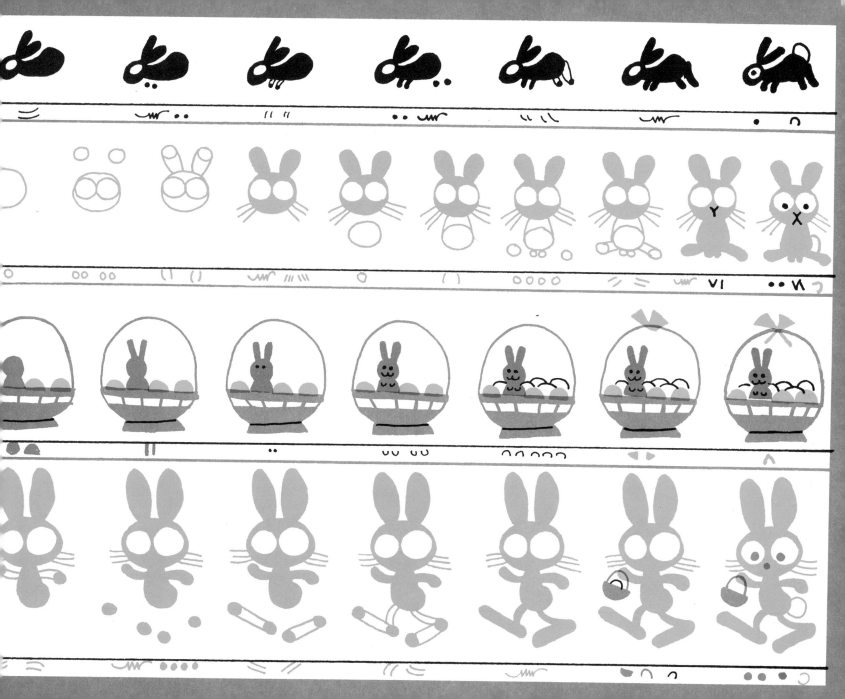

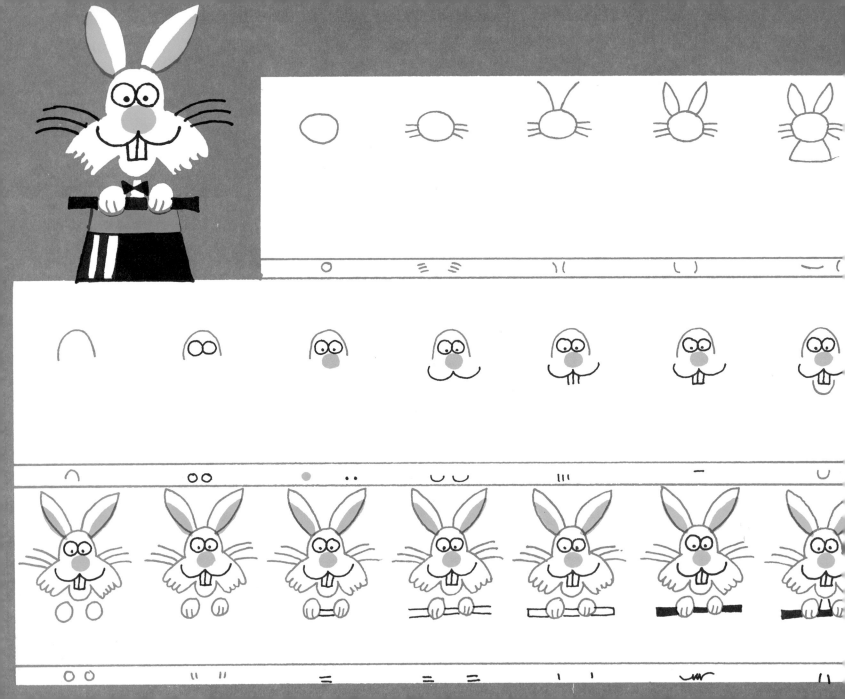

ALSO

ALSO

THE STORK

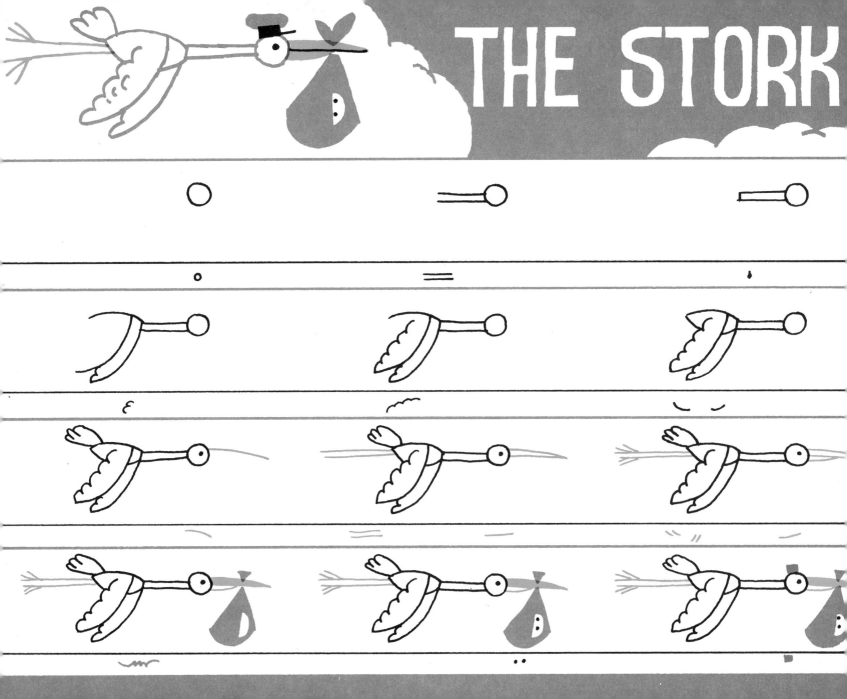

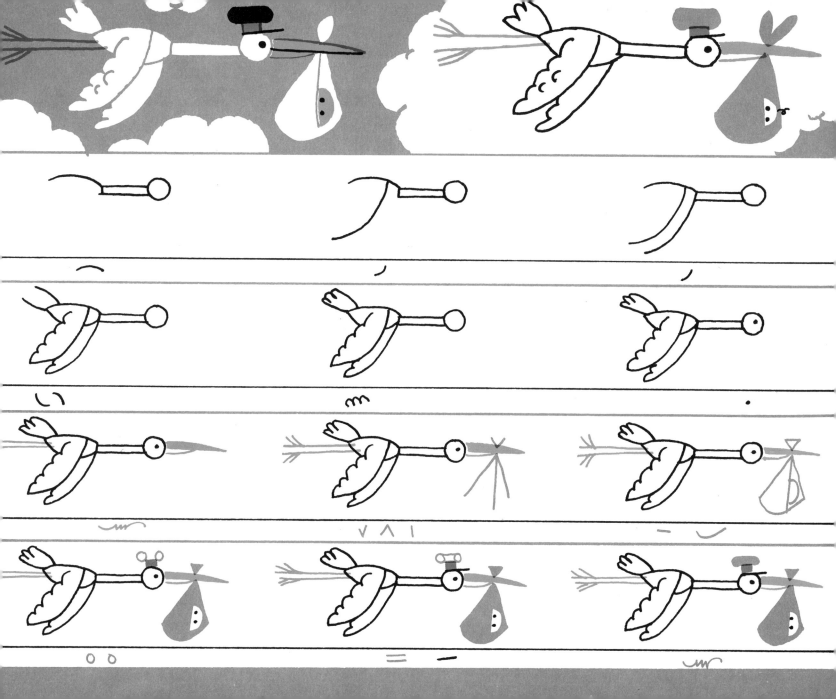

WALRUS

WINKING   SLEEPY   SUNGLASSES   HAT AND TIE

BEAVERS

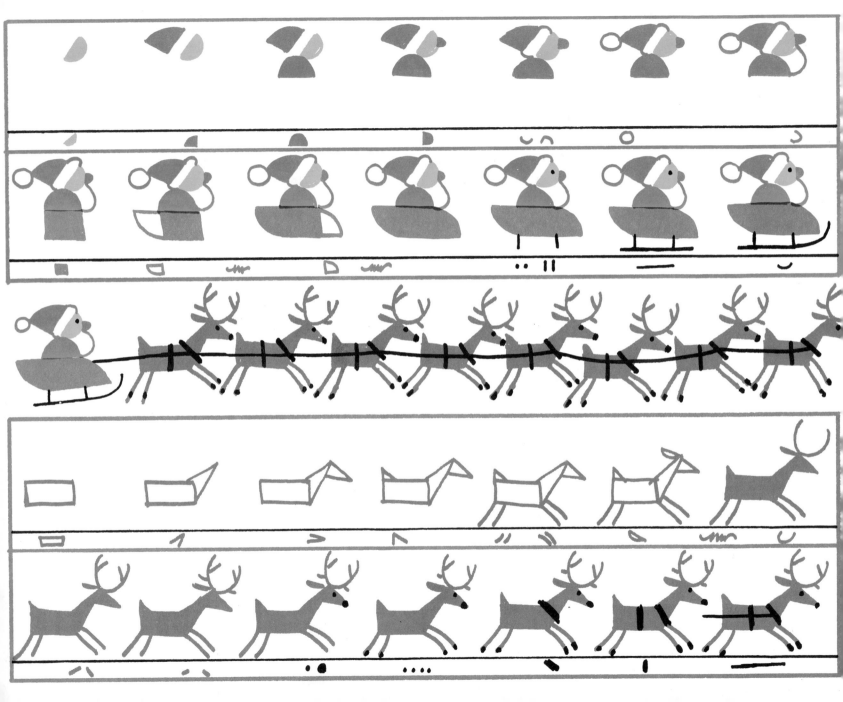

RED and GREEN

"Just-right" colors for
drawing Santa Claus
and Christmas trees.

CHRISTMAS ♪ TREE ♪ OH ♪ CHRISTMAS ♪ TRE

BASIC

V BOTTOM

RAGGED BOTTOM

ALSO

HERE ARE A FEW SIMPLE TREES
FOR YOU TO DRAW AND DECORATE.

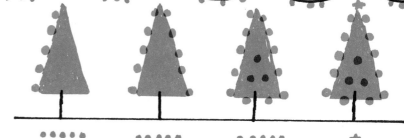

| LARGE STAR ∧ ⋏ ⋆ ☆ ★ | ←THIS IS THE WAY I USUALLY DRAW A STAR...BUT WHEN THE STAR IS VERY SMALL AND THE MARKER IS VERY THICK I DRAW A STAR THIS WAY→ | SMALL STAR ∧ ⋆ |

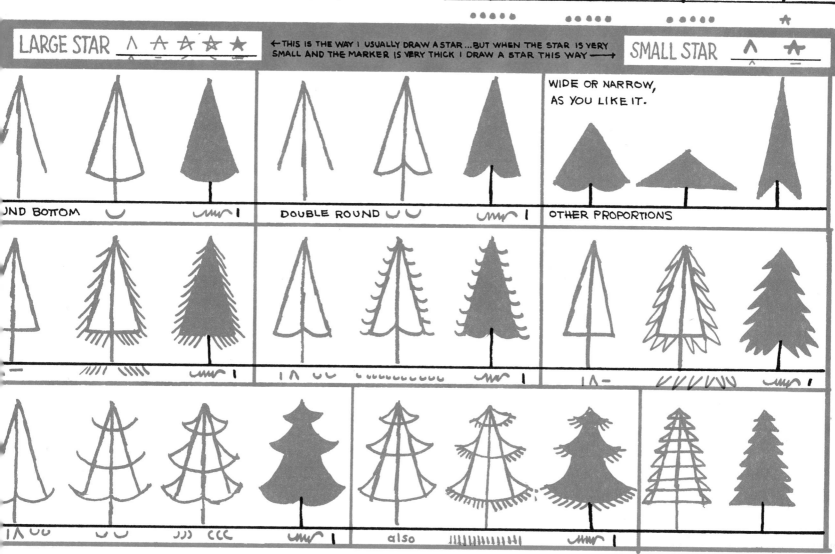

ROUND BOTTOM

DOUBLE ROUND

WIDE OR NARROW, AS YOU LIKE IT.

OTHER PROPORTIONS

also

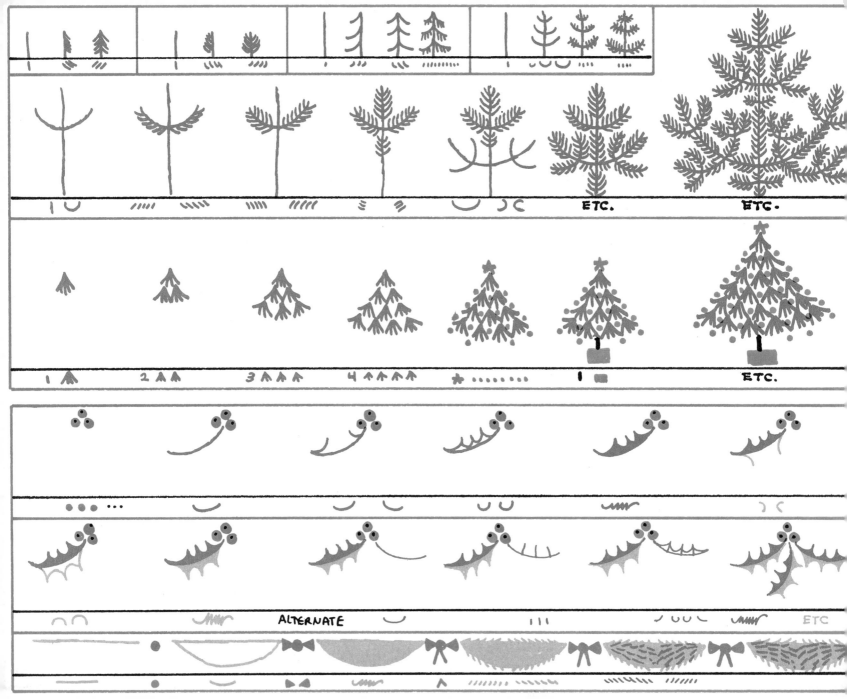

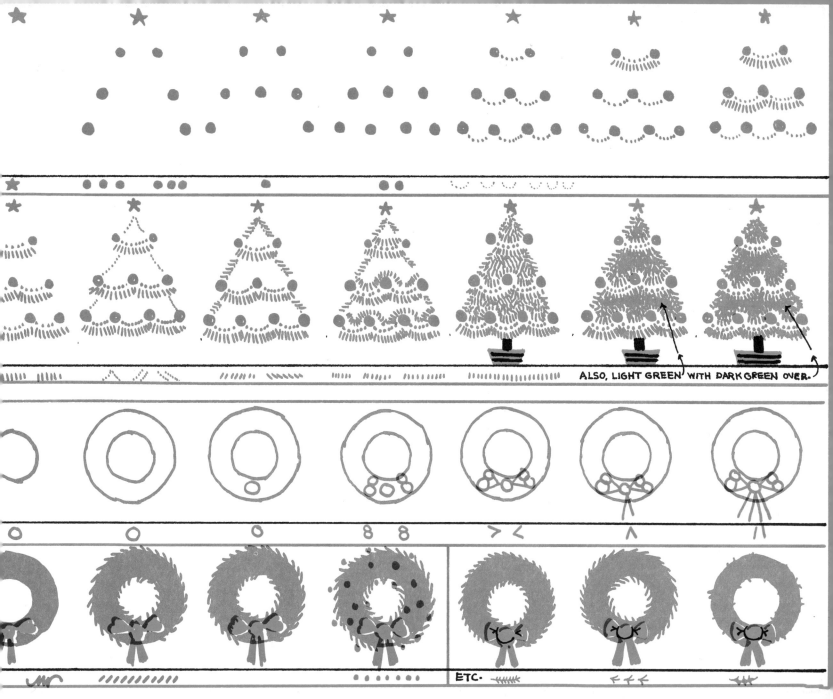

ALSO, LIGHT GREEN WITH DARK GREEN OVER.

ETC.

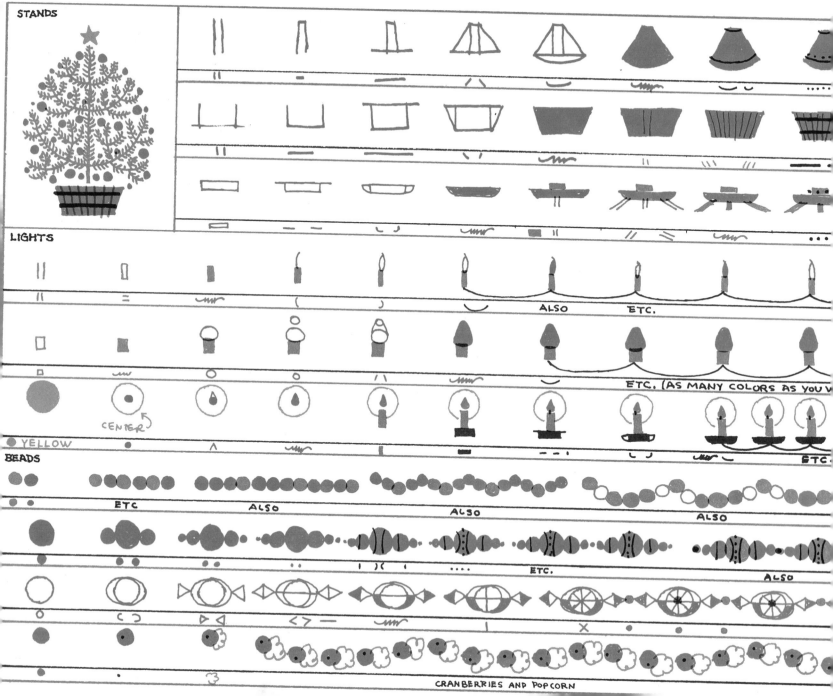

STANDS

LIGHTS

YELLOW

BEADS

ETC   ALSO   ALSO   ALSO

ALSO

CENTER

ALSO

ETC

ETC.

CRANBERRIES AND POPCORN

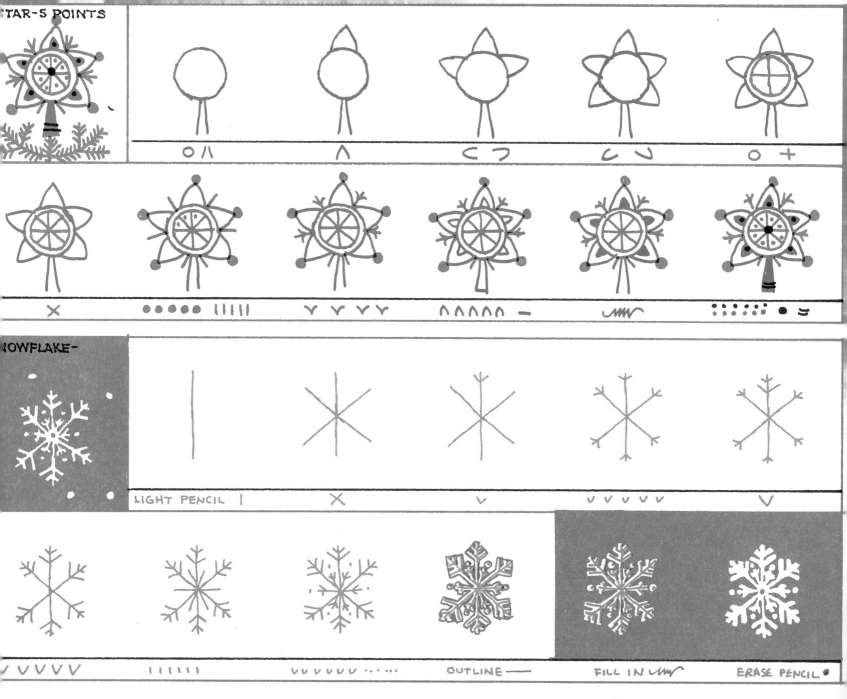

STAR-5 POINTS

○ /\   /\   ⊂ ⊃   ∪ ∪   ○ +

✕   ●●●●● ||||| Y Y Y Y   ∧∧∧∧∧ —   ⌣⌣⌣   :::::·· ● ⹀

SNOWFLAKE-

LIGHT PENCIL | ✕   ∨   ∨∨∨∨∨   ∨

∨∨∨∨∨ |||||| ∪∪∪∪∪ ·····   OUTLINE ——   FILL IN ⌇⌇   ERASE PENCIL ●

DECORATIONS

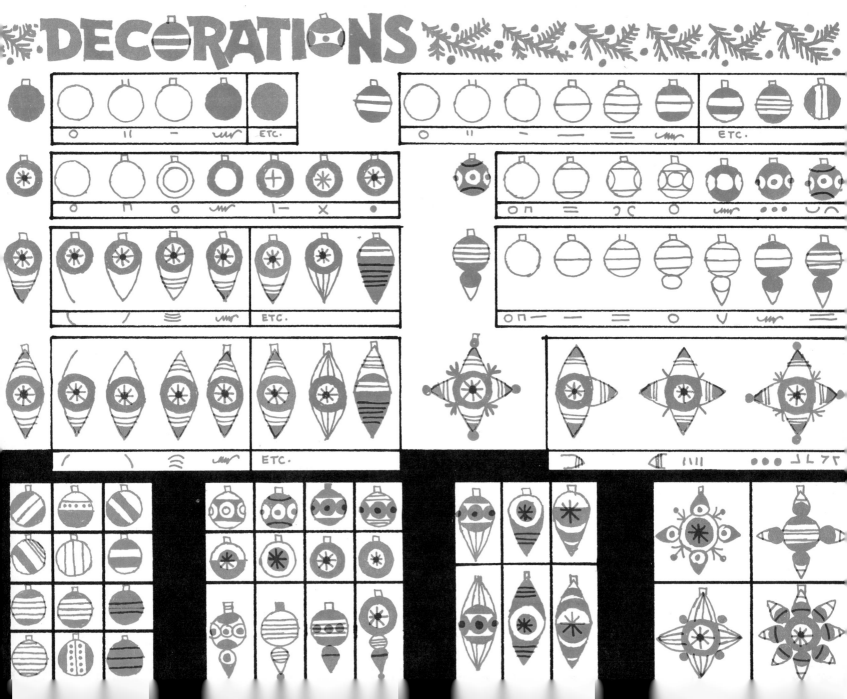

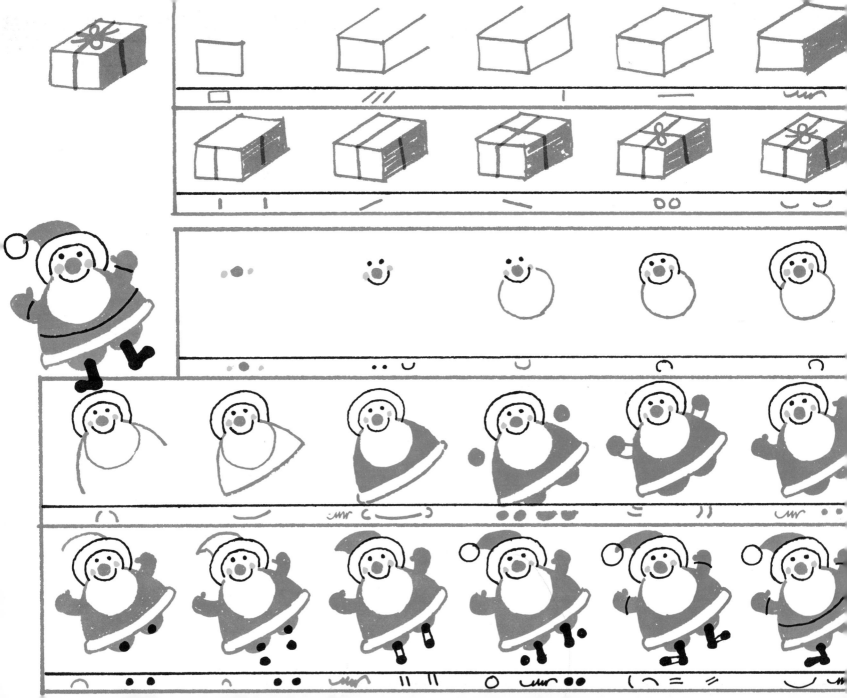

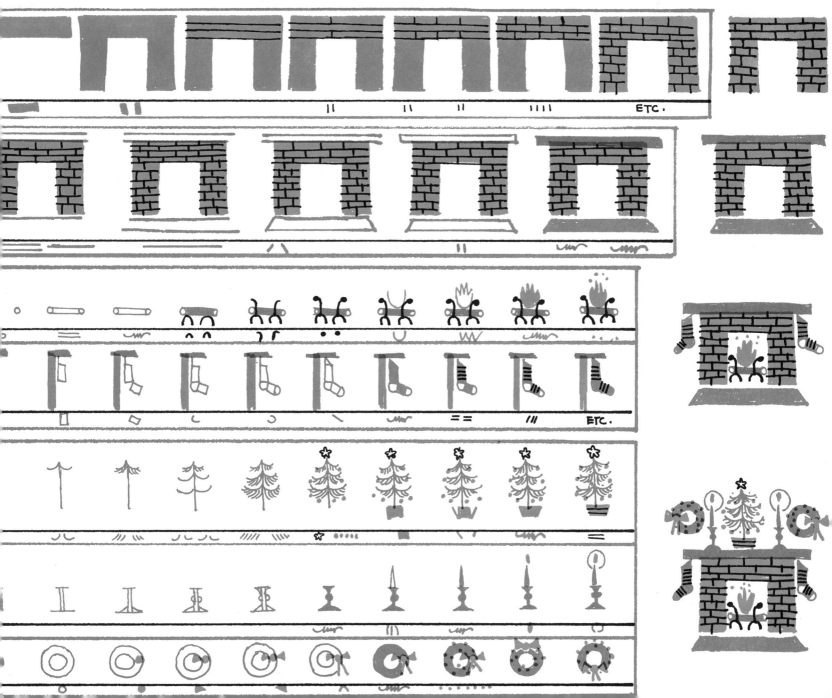

ETC.

ETC.

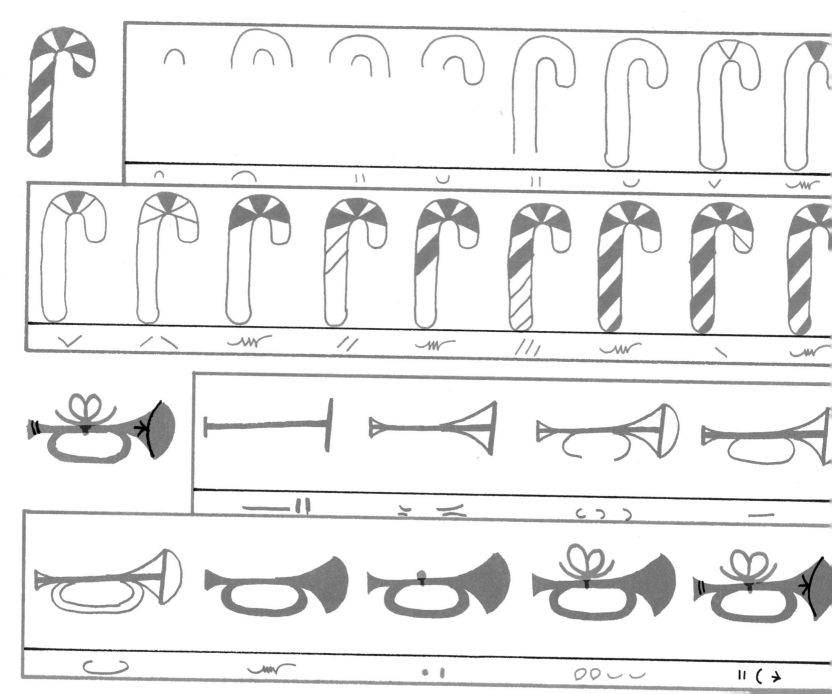

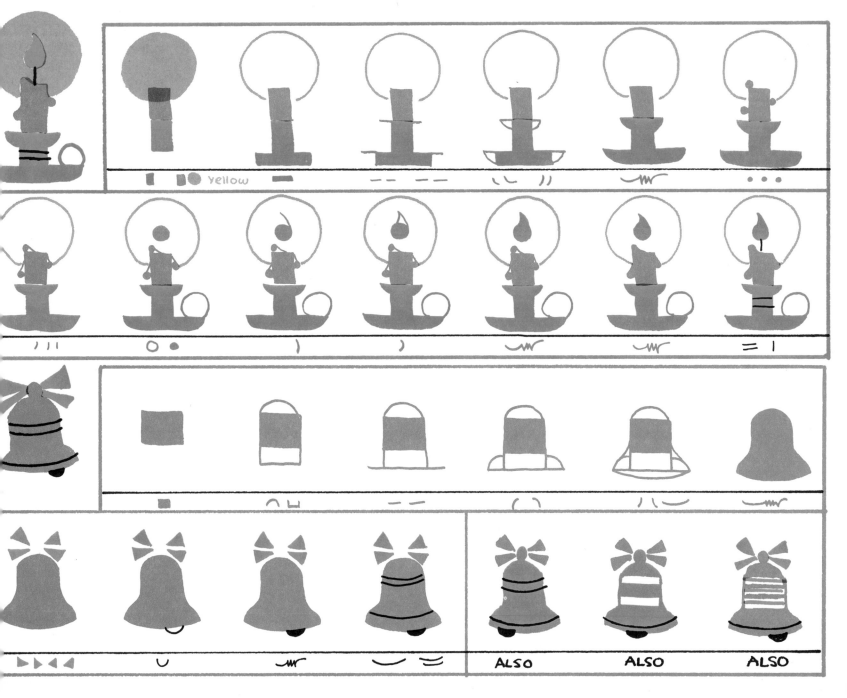

yellow

ALSO   ALSO   ALSO

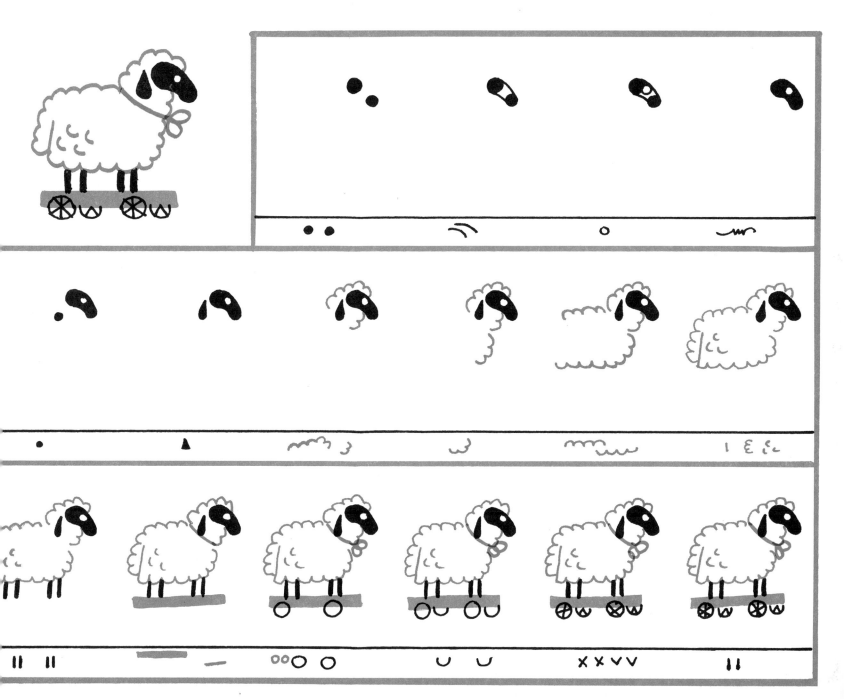

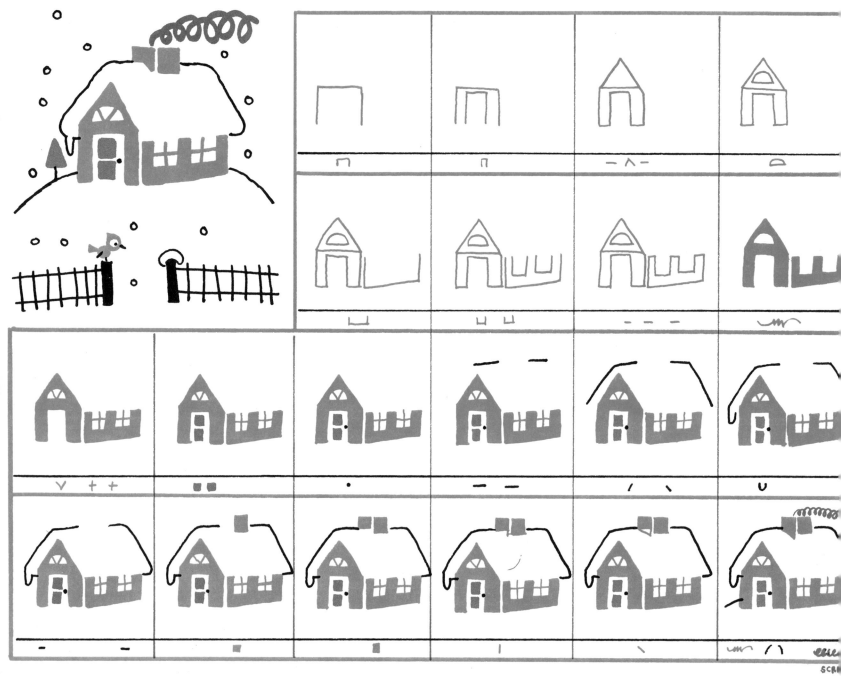

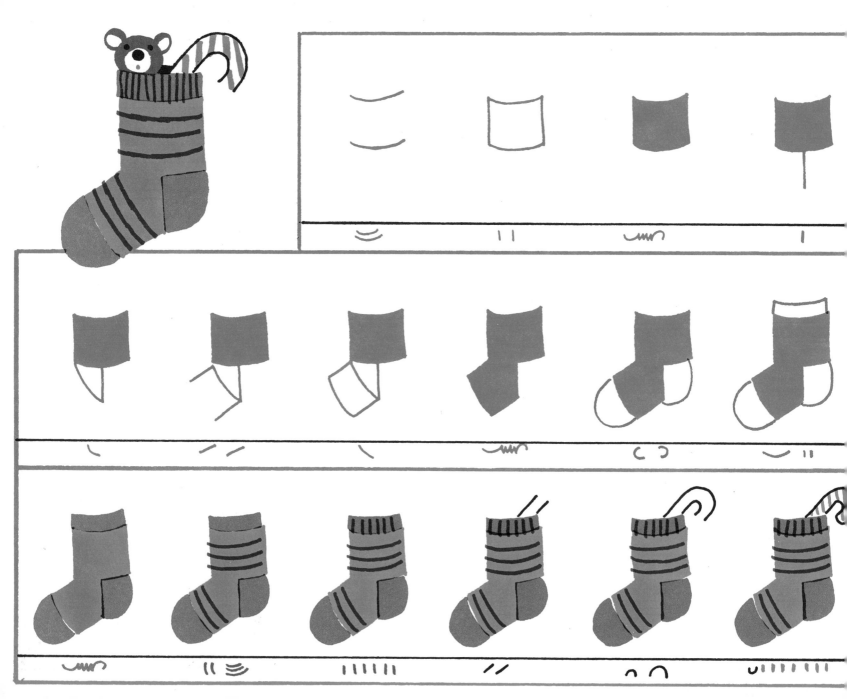

TO MAKE THIS BEAR LOOK FUZZY, USED A DOTTED LINE

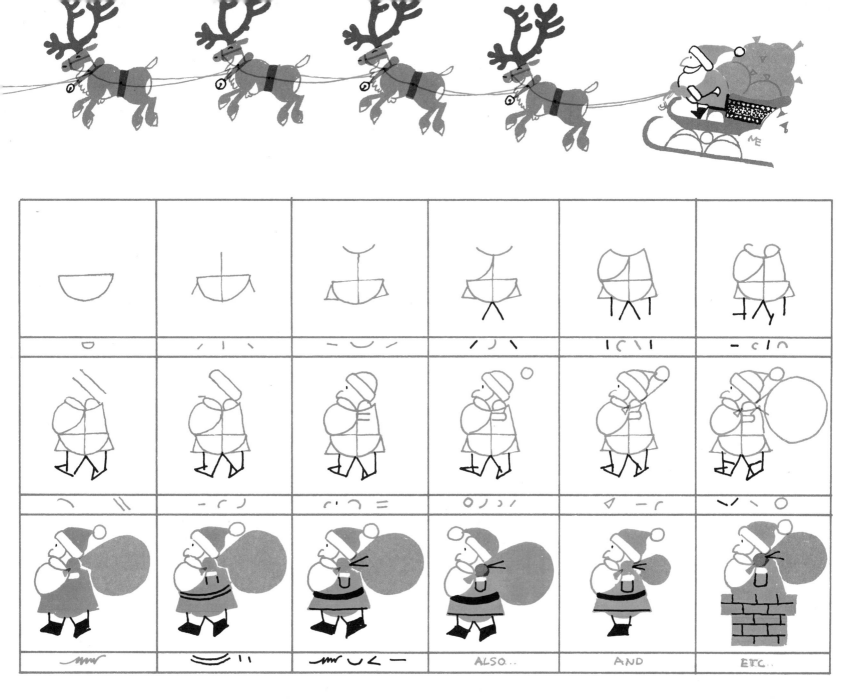

ALSO...

AND

ETC...

ALSO

AND

ETC.   M

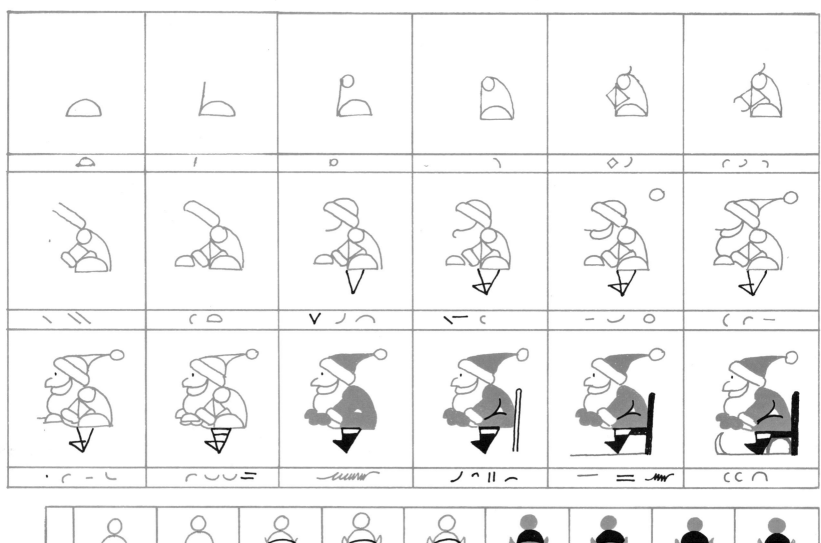

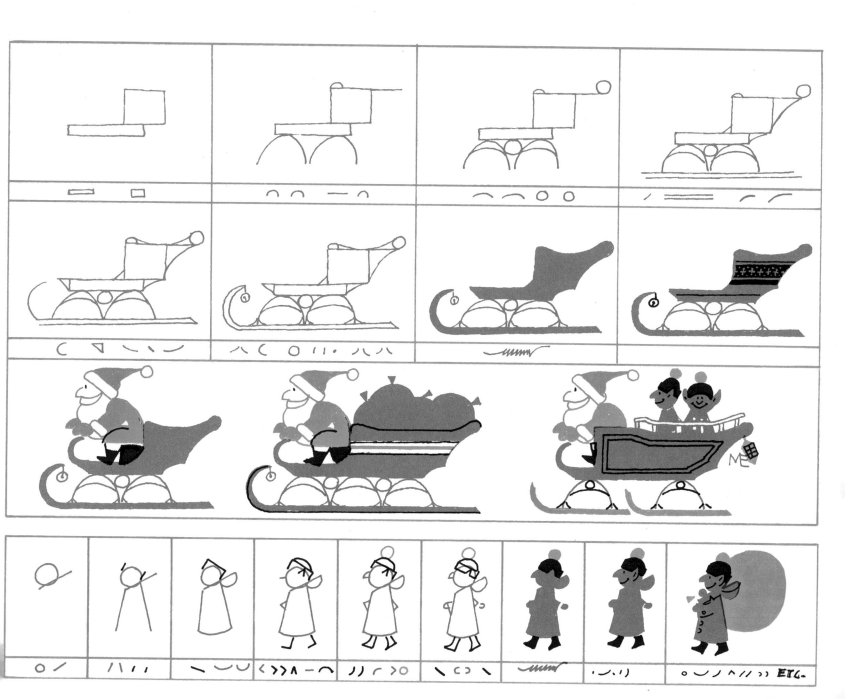

EMBERLEY FAMILY TRIVIA
  FATHER — ED DREW THE PICTURES
  DAUGHTER — REBECCA DREW THE INSTRUCTIONS

SON — MICHAEL, GUEST ARTIST (LOOK FOR HIS MARK ME)

GRANDDAUGHTER — ADRIANNE ENTERTAINED US ALL
DURING THE 1,000 OR SO HOURS IT
TOOK TO FINISH THIS BIG RED DRAWING BOOK